VOICES FROM JERUSALEM

Studies in Judaism and Christianity

*Exploration of Issues in the
Contemporary Dialogue Between
Christians and Jews*

Editor in Chief for
Stimulus Books
Helga Croner

Editors
Lawrence Boadt, C.S.P.
Helga Croner
Leon Klenicki
John Koenig
Kevin A. Lynch, C.S.P.

 A STIMULUS BOOK

VOICES FROM JERUSALEM

Jews and Christians Reflect on the Holy Land

Edited by
David Burrell and Yehezkel Landau

A STIMULUS BOOK
PAULIST PRESS ♦ NEW YORK ♦ MAHWAH

Library of Congress Cataloging-in-Publication Data

Voices from Jerusalem: Jews and Christians reflect on the Holy Land/edited by David Burrell and Yehezkel Landau.
        p. cm.—(Studies in Judaism and Christianity) (A Stimulus book)
   Includes bibliographical references and index.
   ISBN 0-8091-3270-2 (paper)
     1. Palestine in Judaism.   2. Palestine in Christianity.   3. Jewish-Arab relations—
   Religious aspects.   I. Burrell, David B.   II. Landau, Yehezkel.   III. Series.
   BM729.P3V65   1991
   261.2'6—dc20   91-22341
                                                                                   CIP

Published by Paulist Press
997 Macarthur Boulevard
Mahwah, N.J. 07430

Printed and bound in the United States of America

Contents

Preface

Yehezkel Landau and David Burrell, C.S.C.

The authors who have joined us in creating this book have sought to shed new light on some perennial questions coloring relations between Jews and Christians:

- What is holiness, and where is it manifest—in history, in special places or entire countries, in the lives of individuals and communities . . . ?

- Is there a particularly Jewish, or Christian, understanding of holiness? If so, how can others who are not members of that faith community relate to its definition of the sacred?

- How should we interpret the name "Israel"? Is it a reference solely to the Jewish descendants of the patriarch Jacob, who was given this name? Or is it a broader, more inclusive term for the people of God, regardless of national origin? What about the traditional Christian claim to have inherited the name and to be the "new Israel"?

- What does the association of "Israel" with a particular land, and now, once again, with a sovereign Jewish community in that land, mean for Jews and for Christians?

The voices represented here are those of Jews and Christians who have spent many years in the holy land. What they have to say, based on their experience, may help others who look at developments there from

1

afar and wonder what they could signify, especially from a faith perspective.

The reestablishment of a sovereign Jewish commonwealth—with a Jewish majority and Christian, Muslim, and other minorities—is not only a quantitative demographic reversal. Qualitatively, the Jewish assumption of political power, and the adjustment by Christians and Muslims to minority status, forces all of us to rethink old assumptions and beliefs. Perhaps Marcel Dubois, one of our authors, best exemplifies the radical change in existential frames of reference. He often introduces himself by saying: "As a Dominican priest, I am a son of the inquisition; now I teach Augustine and Aquinas to Jews, in Hebrew, at the Hebrew University in Jerusalem." From the Jewish side, the sense of security and of being-at-home that derives from Israeli citizenship allows for a greater degree of mutuality and trust than existed, especially in Jewish-Christian relations, before 1948.

The ongoing conflict in the holy land between Israeli Jews and Palestinian Arabs, often exacerbated by competing religious claims, makes each of these questions more than a purely theoretical matter. The suffering of many people, and the prospect for relieving that suffering, are directly related to how we answer these questions.

The Middle East conflict has also had its impact on the content of this book. Our original intention was to include an essay by a Palestinian Christian. Several Palestinian priests and religious educators were asked to write a chapter, but in the end none of them felt able to contribute an essay to this anthology. So, instead, we have included a sensitive and cogent analysis of "The Crisis of Palestinian Christians" by Fr. Peter Du Brul of Bethlehem University.

Limiting our purview to Christian-Jewish relations means that a Muslim voice is absent from these pages, though one of us has addressed the Islamic connection to Hebron and Jerusalem. With the obstacles inherent in the current political climate, it is doubtful whether a Palestinian Muslim would have agreed to appear in print along with our Israeli authors.

Having acknowledged what this anthology lacks, we offer it convinced that the testimonies which are included will help to clarify some critical issues impacting on Jewish-Christian relations in our time. Shahé Ajamian's Armenian Orthodox perspective, for example, should help western Catholics and Protestants appreciate how faith, peoplehood, and land can co-exist as integral elements of a religious identity. Jewish self-understanding has long been characterized by such a tripartite identification, yet many Christians have difficulty relating to what seems to be a restrictive attachment to territory and nationality. A different Christian approach may yield some new insights on this subject. The Epilogue addresses the commonalities linking Armenians, Jews, and Palestinians and asks whether the pluralistic geography of Jerusalem's Old City, with separate quarters for each of these three communities, may not serve as a model for reconciling diversity with universality.

The structure of the book reflects the spatial and temporal dimensions of identity as defined through faith. Geography and history are not only identity coordinates for the human personality; they are also loci for holiness, and are so addressed from both Jewish and Christian viewpoints. The essay by Simon Schoon surveys the various forms of Christian presence and witness in the holy land today. Also treated is the Israeli-Palestinian dispute, and how nationalism and religion are interconnected factors in that dispute. The essays by Uriel Simon and Peter Du Brul offer some critical distance on the flood of news reports from the Middle East. Examining the underlying issues from a deeper faith perspective can help one cope with the frustration and despair that may be engendered by the tragic developments in the holy land. The Epilogue tries to weave some of these earlier themes together, focusing on Hebron and Jerusalem as holy centerpoints with the potential for promoting reconciliation.

As co-editors, we are gratified that this volume appears in the STIMU-LUS series issued by Paulist Press. We are especially grateful to Helga Croner for her patience and understanding throughout this project. During the course of preparing the book, two of the authors completed their allotted time among us. We feel bereft at their passing, for André Neher and Pinchas Peli were extraordinarily gifted intellects and teachers. May this volume, dedicated to them both, serve as a modest memorial to their exemplary lives of faithful service in the Lord's vineyard.

Introduction: How Christians Share in the Destiny of Israel

David Burrell, C.S.C.

Once upon a time someone proposed that Jerusalem be considered an international enclave administered by the United Nations. And for part of that time a similar proposal even enjoyed Vatican support. Yet anyone who tried to imagine such a suggestion would find it either ludicrous or a comic gesture of despair: if not the Turks, maybe the U.N. For the proposal directly counters our collective experience about political administration, yet what may have made it sound acceptable for Jerusalem is the very chaos of the city itself.

No reflection on Jerusalem can gainsay the fact that the city has no center. The Western Wall, the Holy Sepulchre, and the Dome of the Rock offer symbolic gathering points for each of the religious communities which revere the city. Yet the fact that they are distinct both underscores my point and makes co-existence possible. So the city's not having a center is what allows it to continue to be holy to three groups whose histories and doctrinal claims have often pitted one against the other. Yet what does stand as the center for Christians—the Holy Sepulchre—also testifies daily to the divisions within Christianity, so even an acknowledged center is not securely so. It took the Turks, after all, to impose that modicum of order known as "the status quo."

Yet without a center itself, the city has been celebrated as the center of the earth since David's psalms, elevated to prophetic visions, informed the medieval Islamic mystic Ibn Ali Ibn Arabi, as well as the author of *The Divine Comedy,* Dante Alighieri.[1] So it is that one is never surprised to meet an acquaintance on the street, since pilgrimage to this holy place

5

comes so naturally, especially to western Christians. And as for those who live here, they are inevitably caught up in its inexplicable attraction—especially so when they have chosen to live here, as many Christians over the ages have in fact chosen. If asked why they are here, they would tend to respond—without pretending to comprehend the answer—that they were bearing witness. A multitude of individuals representing various groups and churches, all bearing witness!

A strange notion indeed, especially when Luke 24:47 and Acts 1:8 speak of "beginning from Jerusalem" to "be my witnesses . . . to the ends of the earth." The witnessing assumes specific forms of service, to be sure: hospices for the aged, retarded, handicapped, deaf, crippled and blind, as well as schools, hospitals and even universities. Yet why here? Because this is the holy land and Jerusalem is the holy city. The expression "holy land" seems to have first been used by Cyril of Scythopolis, a monastic author describing the golden age of Palestinian Christianity during the sixth century.[2] And the reference is expressly ambiguous, for what made the land holy was certainly the presence of thousands of monks in the Judean desert regions and throughout the land—yet their very coming also reflected a mysterious attraction to this very place where the Lord had lived.

So the idea of "bearing witness" in Jerusalem is not really an *idea* at all, but represents a concrete human response to what faith presents as an astounding fact of history: that "the Word was made flesh" *here.* Nothing more, really, need be said to explain a Christian presence here. It is heartening, of course, to see that presence manifested in works shaped by the gospels themselves: serving the blind, lame, lepers, the deaf and the poor (Lk 7:22)—heartening, especially, when one is confronted with the stark counter-witness of the crusades, themselves also rooted, no doubt, in that same felt reaction to the startling facts grounding Christianity. Indeed, the current mosaic of Christian communities and works in the holy land seems to reflect a semi-conscious fresh start on the part of the ostensibly Christian nations of Europe to establish, in the last century, a *pied-à-terre* in Jerusalem.

Such is the collective Christian witness in Jerusalem. Besides the spectrum of religious communities spawned by western Catholicism, and the broad variety of Protestant churches familiar to us, the full panoply of eastern Christianity is present as well, with each of them enjoying an historical precedence nearly eclipsing that of the western churches. Armenians, Copts and Ethiopians, as well as Syrians, Chaldeans and Greek Orthodox communions are each represented, as well as the congregations within those communities which have chosen to affiliate with Rome, the best known of which would be the Melkites and the Maronites. And what sort of witness does this presence of so many different historic communities give? It is difficult to answer that question, of course, since a witness must be received to be realized. What Christian visitors most often take home with them is quite negative: the scandal of division and lack of cooperation among the communities. What others, including Israelis, see is something quaint and colorful, reminiscent of another age. One fact stands out above all: it is in no wise an authentically collective witness.

In fact, one could argue that, despite the obvious good being done, the witness of the pluriform Christian communities is hardly evangelical, since they fall so easily into political camps and are generally so ill-prepared to work for reconciliation in a land which cries for it. Excuses abound, of course, and are perfectly understandable. To participate in the colorful Palm Sunday procession from the Mount of Olives into Stephen's (Lion's) gate, amidst religious sisters and brothers shepherding the children they teach, readily explains why most Christians serving in the land are pro-Arab. So would anyone be—Jew, Christian or Muslim—if he or she daily taught Arab children or served their families in clinics. And if we add to our natural sympathy for the less fortunate the gospel's preference for those whom the dominant society has marginalized, the die is cast. As for those western Christians uncritically enthusiastic about Israel, their position is less comprehensible, since it stems not from pastoral concern but from a questionable theology which easily hardens into an ideology. Yet their actions remain consistent with a set of beliefs which links the state of Israel so closely with biblical prophecy as to exempt its actions from ordinary scrutiny

From that same Bible and gospel, however, those explanations are but excuses. For the person and message of Jesus must retain sufficient freedom from specific political options to give them direction. What distinguishes revelation from political consensus is the capacity to continue to render judgment, even on those endeavors undertaken in its name. Indeed, one is tempted to say *especially* on those: Does a Christian institution actually witness to the gospel? Is a Jewish endeavor faithful to the Torah? When we forbid ourselves to ask these questions, we betray the very names we have used. And a so-called theology which justifies our complacency has, in fact, become an ideology.

These distinctions are important if we are to render an accurate account of our witness: for one is called upon to witness to something and to someone. As a result, I can never simply describe what I am doing as witnessing, but am always challenged to give an account faithful to the object of my witness. And beyond that—difficult enough when one must say "the gospel"—I must always be ready to hear that my way of witnessing has failed to communicate, or even conveyed a contrary message.

So one is doubly vulnerable when one's actions purport to be a witness. Yet such is the risk of Christian discipleship, so no one can escape rendering an account of oneself or facing the scrutiny of others. My contention will be that the witness of Christians in Israel has been decisively affected by the ingathering of the Jewish people to this land, and that someone desiring to be a disciple of Jesus has no choice but to support both peoples. One must support Israel because God "does not repent of the gifts he makes or of the calls he issues," and the connection of God's people with this land is of more than historical significance.[3] And one must support the Palestinians, since their human rights to a home and to equal dignity and respect form the background for Jesus' teaching manifest in the Hebrew scriptures as well as the "natural law" tradition.[4] In each case, of course, one's being for a party in a contest cannot mean that one supports that "side" uncritically. Nor should anyone be asked to render "support" of that kind, since uncritical friends are hardly trustworthy. And this would be especially true for Christian discipleship, which must always remain open to the judgment of the gospel.

I shall defend my contention regarding the theological significance of the ingathering, as well as its practical consequence: that Christians in this land will inevitably find themselves between two peoples and hence challenged to a work of reconciliation. But first an observation about the locale, related to the fact that Jerusalem has no center. It consists, rather, of contiguous worlds whose practical overlap affects them hardly at all. The visitor's map of the old city indicates four quarters within the walls: Christian, Muslim, Jewish, and Armenian. So it is, and has been for centuries. The Galilee, too, is checkered with Arab villages, kibbutzim and moshavim (Jewish collective farms and villages), with only a modicum of mixed populations even in a larger city like Haifa. The Middle East has known similar patterns for centuries, and managed to live with them better than we would think possible—but only because there is, in fact, so little actual communication between contiguous communities.

One feature of this pattern of living can give us some hope: people who grow up within it develop quite extraordinary skills of co-existence. One is always faced with the prospect of a war for turf, of course, especially given the presence of adolescent males. Yet even here, as societies generate iron-clad, if informal, rules for interaction, they can do the same for refraining from mixing. Moreover, such is the Middle Eastern pattern, doubtless reinforced by a thousand years of Islam, with its special laws for minorities. This simple yet sturdy fact is heartening because it means that the Middle East does have resources for dealing with potential conflicts quite unsuspected in the west. We need not feel compelled to find our kind of "solution" for the situation. On the other hand, it obviously limits perspectives as well, for "where one stands depends on where one sits." The de facto residential segregation in American cities, reinforced by real estate practices and neighborhood associations, gives us a ready example. To appreciate how the "other" feels, one must live among them, and all the normal conventions prohibit just that to all but a few. Here, too, church becomes one of the few vehicles, if not the only one, for spanning different worlds.

And worlds they are and become, with all the normal fears about venturing into the "other one." The best illustration I know was a one-year student at the Hebrew University who came from Saint Mary's College, Notre Dame, Indiana. Since one of her fellow students (from St. Mary's) lived in Jerusalem, she made contact with her friend's Arab family on arrival and made a point of visiting her mother during the year, especially after the daughter had returned to continue her studies in America. As a result, she regularly found herself correcting misconceptions bandied about among her friends in the one-year program at Hebrew University about "Arabs." For, in fact, they had never met any in a natural family setting, since the program is designed to introduce young men and women to Israel. And Israel, it seems, does the best it can to overlook its Arab population—which is precisely what happens as separate worlds consolidate. Yet when this is reinforced by an historic Jewish separateness and aggravated by a presumptive western superiority, the systematic overlooking can harden into a collective deception: there are no Arabs! Or what are they doing here anyway? (The absence of Jewish communities in most Arab countries completes the mutual separation.)

And when that self-deception affects official policy, it hardens into a political lie. Like the manifest contradiction between the Declaration of Independence and the subsequent stipulation in the United States Constitution that slaves counted as $\frac{2}{3}$ persons, a society is driven to violence to keep such contradictions from surfacing as a lie. And so we have the age-old degeneration of fears into violence, abetted by stereotypes and collective deceptions on each side, which harden before long into lies. These must never be acknowledged to be lies, however, so the informal workings of society as well as the formal apparatus of the state must keep them from emerging as untruth. Yet since truth has uncomfortable ways of asserting itself—in children's questions and young adults' impatience with incongruities—those systems must work constantly to "keep up appearances," sometimes to the point of restraining "offenders." So runs a particularly perceptive account of the roots of violence, which recommends itself especially to each of us who can recognize it at work in our respective lives and cultures.[5] It should be easy to see, moreover, that a society so segregated as the Middle East, and particularly Jerusalem, would be especially vulnerable to such a degenerative process. That is the less hopeful side of the checkerboard pattern, and indicates an area where western skills, as well as Christian convictions, may have a notable role to play.

My own experience in this land has been particularly serendipitous in bridging these all-too-settled worlds. It began with a thorough introduction to the three religious cultures and histories through a summer Hope Seminar in 1975 designed by Sister Marie Goldstein. We lived together for seven weeks—Jews, Christians, and Muslims—studying each religious tradition for two weeks at a time, and culminating with a desert experience in the Sinai. Friendships from that time have lasted for over a decade, and the understanding I gained there of the *Shabbat* decisively shaped my entire approach to prayer and to celebrating the day of the Lord. When I returned in 1980 to serve as rector of the Ecumenical Institute for Theological Research (Tantur), I realized from the outset that my primary task would be one of bridging worlds.

Tantur's location—between Jerusalem and Bethlehem and readily accessible to both—gives to those coming there an ideal location from which to feel the tensions of this land. For one sits between the two worlds, and so must at least try to stand in both of them. The pain one soon feels at absorbing the fear and anger of each side as they speak about the "others" is augmented when one counts personal friends among those others. And more often than not I was dining with *them* the night before, or had been with *them* for lunch that same day. It is hardly a comfortable position, and all those informal rules of polite behavior advise one to "change one's tune" appropriately, yet that will not do. It will not do precisely because I may well be their only trustworthy contact with "the other side." A colleague teaching philosophy at Bir-Zeit University (on the West Bank) was especially grateful for an invitation to west Jerusalem, for he was acutely aware that his only experience with Israelis was with uniformed young men carrying automatic rifles. I could tell him that I looked at them differently after I had met two of them at *Shabbat* eve supper in their family circle. Yet if we admit that setting to be the more natural one, we must also acknowledge that his experience was more typical than mine of people in his society. Whichever the world into which one is inserted, there is little chance to meet the other at home. Hence the immense task of bridging the worlds.

And then in 1981–82 I lived at Isaiah House, a French Dominican *maîson d'études* expressly founded to work with the Jewish people. There we prayed the church's daily prayer (comprised principally of psalms) in Hebrew, and my studies in Jewish and Islamic philosophy carried me into both Hebrew and Arabic. Besides sharing the fruit of that study in a seminar at the Hebrew University, I directed a theological reflection session on selected topics in Judaism and Christianity at the Ratisbonne Center for Studies and Documentation on Judaism, and participated in similar discussions through the Ecumenical Fraternity for Theological Research and the Rainbow Club (the latter being a monthly gathering of Jewish and Christian scholars). So my entire context, if you will, has been Israel, yet that fact has only reinforced my thesis about the contiguous worlds. For in countless conversations I had to insist: It simply is not like that over there. And we were but a ten-minute walk from east Jerusalem!

How can theology help to bridge such a gap? The answer, I believe, rests in people, for there is no theology outside of what theologians actually do. And if I focus on the people with whom I have lived, that has the advantage of presenting individuals for whom living in Israel has made a significant difference in their ways of thinking and of perceiving reality. And it is otherwise difficult to convey a contention that is shared by all who have spent an extended period here, notably at Tantur: one does theology differently in this land. There is, first of all, the palpable presence of history, which renders abstract questions of "historicity" quite superfluous. And there is the equally palpable presence of a Jewish majority, which fact alone upsets a cultural dynamic prevailing over the last nineteen centuries anywhere on the globe.

It was that second fact which motivated the three French Dominicans with whom I lived to leave their homeland for Israel over twenty years ago. The initiator of Maîson Saint Isäie is of Jewish descent, from the international milieu of Cairo between the two world wars. The other two, of solid Catholic stock, heard early on some mysterious call to cast their lot with Israel. Bruno Hussar, the founder of Isaiah House, and a key figure in the Vatican II statement on the Church and the Jewish people, has moved on to establish a community for reconciliation among Jews and Arabs in what had been a portion of no-man's-land from 1948 to

1967. His earliest collaborator, Jacques Fontaine, was led by his love for the land to become a licensed guide, and continues to weave a detailed grasp of terrain and history into a concrete appreciation of the scriptures for those adventurous enough to follow his program of *Bible sur terrain*. The last, Marcel Dubois, is recently retired from his position as senior lecturer in philosophy at the Hebrew University, where he has introduced generations of students into Greek and medieval philosophy, and explored Aquinas with those prepared and willing. He also brings considerable personal, as well as intellectual, presence to many facets of life in Jerusalem.

Each of these men has expressly sought Israeli citizenship, and each displays in his mode of work a commitment to the people and to the land. Bruno Hussar, moved by the prospect of "two justices" unable to make humane contact with one another, has labored to plant an indigenous community of Jews and Arabs—*Neve Shalom*—which can extend its experience of shared living with young people growing up in otherwise separate worlds. The programs sponsored there use multiple means of communication to bring people face-to-face with one another. Jacques Fontaine's integration of the word with the earth gives western Christians and local residents a felt appreciation for that internal connection of land with people which normally poses such an obstacle to Christians' appreciation of Judaism, and especially of Israel. And Marcel Dubois, it is fair to say, has prompted Israelis themselves to reflect on the roots of their adventure by his own moving sense for "the mystery of Israel" (conveyed in his contribution to this volume).

Yet each of these individuals also senses himself to be working alone, in the presence of an opportunity and a challenge so intently ignored by the bulk of Christians in the land, and throughout the world. The opportunity is the ingathering which is Israel, and the challenge is one which would shatter the age-old ideology which Christianity has used to keep Jews "in their place." Israel can be a school for those who would learn— an experimental school, for it continues to be just that. Rather than impose on the fledgling nation their understanding of what its history portends, these men are of a more critical temperament, used to testing the spirit and assaying its fruits. They have let their Christian faith be informed by the patterns which can be embodied in a Jewish society—notably the festivals and the *Shabbat*—yet resolutely eschew mixing forms of expression. Their witness lies in their engagement; the daily prayer draws from its roots to speak in a clear Christian voice. Yet the difference made when the psalms are chanted in Hebrew can hardly be gainsaid. As a monastery has ever been conceived as a "school of the Lord's service," the instruction to be had from this milieu offers a special advantage to searching Christians. And like the monastic pattern, it never ceases to embrace one's life.

The challenge can best be put by reminding oneself of Luther's remark that if the Jews were to reestablish themselves in the holy land, he would be the first to go there and have himself circumcised![6] For it was the diaspora after all, on top of the destruction of the Temple, which served the early church fathers as historical evidence for the superiority of the new covenant over the old. Their overt references to this dual fact were dramatically punctuated by the explosive reaction of Christians to Emperor Julian's proposal to rebuild the sanctuary in Jerusalem in 363. So what the patristic age formulated, medievals and reformers took for granted: that the new law had simply replaced the old.[7] Such a teaching, needless to say, left no breathing room for Judaism except what Jews themselves could furtively set apart. Nor were their temporal rhythms respected either, since Sunday eclipsed the sabbath. Moreover, theological strictures have a way of hardening into political ideologies, so that the world's collective horror at the accounts from Nazi extermination camps caused Christian churches to examine how much their settled teaching about Jews could have lent unwitting support to such unprecedented systematic slaughter.[8]

What the destruction of the Temple and subsequent diaspora were to the church's earliest theologians, Auschwitz and the founding of Israel have been to this generation. Yet the response has been spotty, since there is such a mass of tradition to be overcome, and many of the unspoken assumptions of that teaching have blocked obvious avenues of inquiry. So the negative images of Pharisee and sabbath prevailing throughout the New Testament itself have come under fresh scrutiny, and the general observation that a family quarrel is usually misinterpreted by outsiders has yielded readings of the apostolic writings at once fascinating and spiritually revolutionary.[9] One of the nicer ironies is the simple observation that whoever insists on blaming someone else (the Jews) for the death of Jesus manages to fulfill the Pharisee stereotype to the letter. For by that subterfuge we effectively destroy any hope of the gospel's judgment renewing our minds and hearts.[10]

It seems to be more than coincidence, moreover, that current concern about better understanding the "parting of the ways" parallels a western opening to the spiritual resources of other religious traditions. A seminal article by Karl Rahner, in fact, identifies two transforming thresholds in the history of the Christian movement: the early transition from a Jewish Christianity to the inclusive movement which came to express itself in largely western cultural terms, and the moment in which we now stand, when "the sphere of the Church's life is in fact the entire world."[11] These two transitions theologically eclipse the reformation for all of its shattering effect on European culture, for each of them poses questions to which the prevailing synthesis of faith and culture cannot respond. What is demanded is a new step forward, growing out of an acute awareness by the church of its mission and of the transformation called forth by an utterly new historical situation.

In such crises of self-understanding, the way forward cannot be charted, and often depends on especially creative spirits. And such ones, Peter reminds us, often "make . . . points . . . hard to understand; [indeed] these are the points that uneducated and unbalanced people distort, in the same way as they distort the rest of scripture" (2 Pet 3:16). And so Paul's castigating of those pagans who sought salvation in imitating Jewish practices has long been read as a diatribe against his own people.[12] What Rahner strongly suggests, in fact, is that our current reassessment of the struggle for self-understanding into which Paul plunged the fresh communities of those following "the Way" may offer us specific help in discerning which way we are now to follow in the face of the other religions and cultures of humankind.

At least, I would add, trying to assimilate the consequences of Auschwitz and the return to Israel will force one's theological reflection out of its accustomed European modes. And it is often the case that living in Israel suggests avenues of inquiry that would rarely occur to someone at home in western Europe or North America. If Karl Barth reminded us that "the great remaining ecumenical question is our relations toward Judaism," Karl Rahner has suggested why: nothing else can so effectively prepare us to face the moment to which history—secular and sacred—has brought us.[13] There is little doubt that a literal reading of the stereotypes of the Pharisee led us to jeopardize our own standing with the Lord by adopting an entirely un-Christlike attitude toward his own people. Yet a penetrating realization of that fact, and of the ways in which such a misreading has also misshaped the attitudes of believers for centuries, could well prepare the way for that renewal of heart and of mind which Vatican II set in motion, yet barely began. Facing the question of our relations with the Jews may free us to face the rest of our brothers and sisters throughout the world. And who could have suspected that—except for the central role God has continually asked this recalcitrant people to play!

Such was my experience living in Isaiah House. The engagement with Israel evidenced by the three men whom I have described never amounted to mindless support of state policies; it has, rather, led them to a critical appreciation of their own faith, and given a suppleness to its embrace which testifies to what Rahner supposes. In fact, one might even suggest that this very interplay between their traditional Christian faith and the realities of Israel has given them the rare skills needed to avoid being trapped by ideologies—especially when these are reinforced by human sympathies. Israel remains an ideal to be realized—the mystery of Israel—as well as a fact to be recognized. The peculiar role a Christian might have to play in helping to bring those two together is variously suggested in the three lives I have referred to.

Yet such a task is always arduous and never clear. One thing alone stands out: we may never let ideologies divert our sympathies or attention from the gospel-call to reconciliation. And an earlier theology-turned-ideology allowed us to do just that with the Jewish people: to consider ourselves exempt from Jesus' norms of behavior in thinking about them or dealing with them. The kind of theology which grows out of our daily encounter with people in Israel will perforce be different, and most probably along the lines suggested. It will also, of course, find itself guided by that continuous strain in Christian theology which affirmed a continuity in God's covenants with us. Yet if it is to be true to its name, it will retain its critical edge, and avoid letting the fullness of God's revelation be so skewed by the memories of more recent events as to forget that God's word is destined for all peoples. That fact should keep the new theology from merely reacting to the old, and indicate clearly a Christian's responsibility for promoting reconciliation in this land. Yet since a reconciling word must also be a critical word, such voices may at times be unwelcome to both "sides."

I have spoken so far as a Christian, and of the responsibility of Christians to work for reconciliation in this land. I have noted the small but promising initiative of Bruno Hussar and the community of Neve Shalom: small because ventures in living together must be on a human scale; promising because it exists where little else of its kind does. Yet the work of reconciliation is shared with "all men and women of good will." As co-editor, Yehezkel Landau will address that task from a Jewish and religious Zionist perspective. Zionism, seen as the movement to promote the ingathering, is something to which I could subscribe as a Christian. Yet it can so easily take on a collective face which leaves no room for anyone else in Israel—or anywhere within its ancient boundaries. A consequence of that attitude is to effectively deny human rights to minorities in the name of "national security." Policies of that sort cannot help but be unpalatable to American Jews, who have often led domestic campaigns to assure minorities their civil rights. Those who wage that struggle in Israel need our support. But our position as Christians remains a delicate one: we cannot allow ourselves to be overcome with guilt—felt or imputed— for the wrongs done to Jews in the name of a crucified Jesus. Yet we must recognize and acknowledge those wrongs, and go on to challenge Israel to live up to its venerable tradition of justice. For the separateness at once indigenous to Judaism and reinforced by centuries of "Christian" social patterns leads one plausibly to argue for the "relative necessity of a state of Israel."[14] Yet in a society so easily traumatized by fear, separateness can lead to collective blindness concerning the "other" in one's midst. Certainly part of a Christian's task in the shared work of reconciliation will be to understand, address, and help move people beyond that fear. Then will our presence truly further the destiny of Israel.

NOTES

1. Robert Briffault, *The Troubadors* (Bloomington: Indiana University Press, 1965), p. 175.

2. I am indebted for this information to Robert Wilken, who is currently writing on Cyril and Christianity in the holy land.

3. The quotation is from the Vatican II document *Nostra Aetate,* cited from Helga Croner, ed., *Stepping Stones To Further Jewish-Christian Relations* (New York: Stimulus Books/Paulist Press, 1977), p. 1. The sense of the last expression is taken from Bruno Hussar's personal reflections on more than twenty years in Israel, to be published by Editions du Cerf (Paris): ch. 8, "Je suis juif."

4. "The conflict here is not one between justice and injustice, as each side will invariably present it, but one between two justices"—Hussar, ch. 13, "L'état d'Israel et les arabes palestiniens."

5. René Girard, *Violence and the Sacred* (Baltimore: Johns Hopkins, 1977) and his later *Des choses cachées depuis la fondation du monde* (Paris: Grasset, 1978).

6. Quoted by Heiko Obermann in a lecture delivered in Jerusalem, May 24, 1982.

7. Aquinas offers significant witness to a deeper current here in his explicit contention that there is but one goal for the two "dispensations": *Summa Theologiae,* I–II 91.5.

8. Helga Croner's edition of church statements documents development in this regard since 1948.

9. See the enlightening and specific responses to Rosemary Ruether's *Faith and Fratricide* (New York: Seabury, 1974) compiled by Alan T. Davies, ed., *Antisemitism and the Foundations of Christianity* (New York: Paulist Press, 1979). For a bold, constructive essay, see Paul van Buren, *Discerning the Way* (New York: Seabury, 1980).

10. John Wilkinson puts this as nicely as I have seen it: ". . . to the present writer it seems that past attempts by Christians to interpret the passion in such a way as to condemn modern Jews exemplify the very attitudes the passion narratives were designed to challenge." *Jerusalem as Jesus Knew It* (London: Thames and Hudson, 1978), p. 144.

11. "Towards a Fundamental Interpretation of Vatican II," *Theological Studies* 40 (1979), pp. 716–27, quote at 721. Cf. also my "Jerusalem and the Future of Theological Inquiry," *Yearbook of the Ecumenical Institute for Theological Research* (Tantur) [P.O.B. 19556, Jerusalem], 1981–82.

12. Lloyd Gaston, "Paul and the Torah," in Alan Davies, ed., op. cit.

13. Speaking at the Vatican Secretariat for Promoting Christian Unity in 1966, Karl Barth stated: "Aber wir sollen nicht vergessen, dass es schliesslich nur eine tatsächlich grosse ökumenische Frage gibt: unsere Beziehungen zum Judentum"—*Freiburger Rundbrief* 1976, p. 27.

14. The wording reproduces a subtitle in the statement of the Synod of the Reformed Church of Holland, 1970: "Israel: People, Land, and State," in Croner, *Stepping Stones*, pp. 91–107; cf. p. 103.

The Land as Locus of the Sacred

André Neher

I
ONE BIBLICAL LAND AND THE SACRED CHARACTER OF THE LAND OF ISRAEL

It is commonly held that the Jewish people's greatest distinction lay in giving the world a God. And we should add: a land. For the singularity of the idea of divinity, revealed through Judaism, is equaled only in the idea of the land, also developed in the matrix of Jewish thought and history. In its biblical expression, the navel of the universe is found in Jerusalem, and the cosmic organism emerges from the embryo of Palestine—or rather, as Jewish tradition would have it, *Erets Israel,* or simply *Erets.* What I hope to elaborate here are the specifically Jewish components of this concept of the single land. They will help us to understand how, for Judaism, Palestine is not merely one element in a sacred geography, but something far more mysterious and intense which holds the key to Jewish existence and to the history of the Jewish people in its most decisive dimensions.

The way the Bible refers to the land is telling. Often it speaks with that tone of admiration which all peoples quite naturally adopt when they try to describe their attachment to their native soil: the beauty of the landscape, the wealth of natural resources, a flourishing culture. Even before the conquest, Moses describes the land in sumptuous language:

> For the Lord your God is bringing you to a rich land, a land of streams, of springs and underground water gushing out in hill and valley, a land of wheat and barley, of vines, fig trees, and pomegranates, a land of olives, oil and honey. It is a land where you will never live in poverty

18

nor want for anything, a land whose stones are iron-ore and from whose hills you will dig copper (Dt 8:7–9).

This country—generous, spacious, worthy of being loved, flowing with milk and honey—will find the reflection of its colors in its monuments and in its cities, as the people take root and grow there. The Song of Songs introduces a whole esthetic scale whose harmonics range from natural features to human achievements: Tirzah, Jerusalem, towers, walls, processions, dances. After many trials we are brought to the more somber tone of certain psalms, redolent of a patriotism tried by fire, where the land is no longer to be loved for its beauty and relics, but for its nudity and misery as well. Dust and rock, elements frankly hostile to humankind, pose an obstacle to civilization and mark the limits of cultural endeavor. And yet we love them desperately, when these are the dust and rock of our homeland:

For thy servants take pleasure in her stones,
and love her dust (Ps 102:14).

Yet this tone is not the most basic one which the Bible evokes with *erets*—a term whose fullness carries connotations well beyond "country" or even "homeland." In the Bible *erets* represents neither a geographical object nor a philosophical abstraction, but a *person*. *Erets* plays its role in the biblical drama alongside God, Israel, and the nations—a primordial role which we shall examine. But we should first note how a particular biblical style displays this feature of *erets*. Not being an object, *erets* is more often invoked than described; we speak to her rather than about her. It would be difficult to find in all of literature a poetic invocation comparable to the celebrated verse of Jeremiah: "*Erets, erets, erets,* hear the word of the Lord" (22:29).

Moreover, as a person, *erets* enjoys the femininity consonant with its grammatical gender: the Bible exploits all of the sympathetic resources which the feminine holds for a poet, as one adored, menacing, evocative. In particular, the sentiment of love finds a natural expression for its countless nuances in the multiple roles which the land plays in the biblical drama. For the roles it plays are essentially feminine: *erets* is the partner who seeks ever to be completed by the other. She cannot live alone; she can be herself only in achieving this union.

Erets forms a primary union with God. *Erets* is the land of God. She is not like Egypt: a land which people trample with their feet. For she is encompassed by the eyes of God; she is turned toward God, offering herself to heaven, drinking from the springs of its rain. This is not a land thoroughly rooted in subterranean strata and finding its nourishment there. It lives from the blessings bestowed on it from God above. There is a continuous dialogue between *erets* and heaven. Unlike other lands, which are all concave, this land opens itself toward heaven in a convex motion of welcome and of receptivity.

But has not God chosen a people as well to assume this posture of welcome and receptivity toward heaven? Israel, unlike the other nations, will be the second companion of this land like no other. Only a people which finds itself at the juncture of the divine and the human can be one with *erets* herself at the juncture of the heavens and the earth.

Only now and again does the Bible mention this double union of *erets* with God and with Israel. It is presented in conjugal language and in a way which allows one to plumb its true meaning. We know how the Bible compares the covenant of God with Israel to a marriage, so licensing Moses, the prophets and the inspired bards of the Canticle and the Psalms to portray the history of this covenant as one of love passing through the most diverse and poignant phases: awakening, first encounter, espousal, union and birth of children, but also jealousy, quarrels, separation, divorce, widowhood, and, finally, passionate return and reconciliation. In this perspective Israel is the female partner of God. But from another perspective, and one closer to reality, Israel is the male partner. Who is the female partner to Israel? *Erets,* of course, the land which waits to be loved and espoused. But here the symbolism once again departs forcefully from reality to attain to a spiritual interpretation, for this land has not been *won* by Israel—contrary to the tenor of the nationalist account with its warrior narratives from the time of Moses and Joshua. Long "promised," she was "offered" by God to Israel. God confided to him this jewel, this precious pearl incubated by God, asking that Israel be the faithful companion of this unique spouse. The pattern for fidelity is carefully traced: it is none other than the Torah, whose scrupulous observance alone can keep the conjugal bonds intact between Israel and *erets.* For God continues to watch over *erets,* even after the marriage, as a father over his favorite daughter. God holds the spouse to obey the elevated spiritual and moral tenets of the Torah; only at that price will he be worthy of *erets.* Otherwise, this land will vomit him forth, as it previously vomited the Canaanites, to whom God had confided it in a moment of hasty imprudence. God will then take back this gift, awaiting—how important a qualification!—

not another people more faithful than Israel, but the repentance of Israel, its return to the Torah and to its vocation as spouse of *erets*.

Such is the biblical theme of the land. Its elements are scattered throughout the Bible in such a way that we may be dispensed from giving the references. A reader familiar with the scriptures will easily recover them, from Leviticus to Isaiah, from Deuteronomy to the Song of Songs. It is a theme which culminates in evoking a land whose space is as indispensable as is the time of human history to the building up of the kingdom of the covenant. In this space, and this space alone, will Israel's destiny be realized, along with the success and the failure of its vocation. *Erets* is the proving ground of election.

II
COSMIC CENTRALITY OF THE LAND OF ISRAEL

One might have thought that the exigencies of exile would have altered, in Jewish thought, the pre-eminence of *erets* and transferred some of its virtues to the lands of the diaspora. In no way. Quite the contrary: from the first centuries of the diaspora, Jewish thought—first talmudic, then philosophical and mystical, and finally political—took up the biblical theme of *erets* in an ever-increasing rhythm, not to dilute it but to endow it with an even greater weight, a more absolute gravity. For if the conversation among God, Israel, and *erets* assumes a dramatic mode in the Bible, and so remains open, indecisive and adventurous, that same conversation acquires in later Jewish thought a hieratic status which no longer conveys a drama so much as a situation. *Erets* is still the privileged land of God, the only place where the Torah can be completely observed, and—as it would soon be said—the only place whose physical and spiritual atmosphere can elicit the gift of prophecy. Only there can tradition and inspiration make themselves felt. Conjugal symbolism is still used in speaking of her, but with a fine nuance: the Zohar would make of *erets* itself the *ketuba*—the marriage contract between God and Israel—and one can see how material and immovable this image makes the presence of the land in the religious economy of Judaism.

The land then assumes a global function. This is especially so since the Jewish conception of things does not separate body from soul, or soul from body. Israel and its land are related as soul and body. We can regard the land as the body of the soul Israel, and Israel as the soul of the body which is the land. We can also speak of the land as the *space* of the time of Israel.

But above all *erets* is the *center*. It is this centrality of Israel which provides the foundation stone for what one can call a "geo-theology" which alone renders the history of the Jewish diaspora comprehensible.

Erets is in fact at the center of the world—a rich enough theme in itself, which is reflected in the work of medieval cartographers. Yet when the discovery of the new world made this theme no longer valid in a purely geographical sense, it remained no less valuable to Jews, for *erets* was less the center of the world than the center of the exile. And the exile never underwent a displacement. On the physical plane, and in a fashion uncontested by science, the exile continued, dispersing the far-flung members of the Jewish people to the four corners of the earth. The centrality of *erets* gave a meaning to the exile which was not an arbitrary dispersion, a formless scattering in space, but a geometric flowering coordinated expressly about a center. As radii converging on a center, the regions of the exile stretched toward *erets*. As far-flung as they may have been, they retained their focus on the center, *erets*. From that center flows the nourishing sap which carries life to the farthest branches; or, better, there can be found the spring of living water feeding the distant canals, and each brook which drinks from this spring knows that one day—in a great cosmic reversal originating not in a new Copernicus or Magellan but in the eternal couple God–Israel—it will reverse its course and will come with all the others to be taken up into the unique spring of *erets*.

The charm of this geo-theology, which takes seriously the most literal biblical prophecies of the return, permeated the most diverse domains during the centuries of the exile. It served to *orient* the community's prayer. For the European Jews, in the strict sense of the word: prayers were directed toward the east, toward the *mizrah* which was a homing star for each synagogue and Jewish home. This conception of a center also ordered the charity of the community, where the fundamental offering was one which reached through various institutions to the poor in *erets*. These were the ones, no matter how far away, identified as the "neighbor" whom one must love, while they in turn, in accepting the donation, helped to confirm the givers in exile in their Jewish vocation. Finally, this charmed center gave to life and death a complementary and harmonious significance. Life in exile was but a slow death, yet burial in *erets* meant access to the resurrection. Whatever stood in the way of Jewish existence in the *galut* was compensated and transmuted by the serene victory of final rest in the holy land. And if logistical difficulties meant that relatively few bodies of Jewish exiles found rest in *erets,* all Jews in exile at least tried to secure a bit of the soil of *erets* for their burial in a strange land.

III
MESSIANIC CHARACTER OF THE LAND OF ISRAEL

All of these attempts to develop and maintain the *erets–galut* polarity are focused and intensified in the larger endeavor to assure an absolute value for *erets.* By intimately linking the biblical "land of holiness" with the exilic conception of *centrality,* Jews arrived at a messianic consciousness of *erets.* Ever since biblical times the messianic idea has been linked to the land of Israel. The messiah will gather the dispersed together in the ancestral land. But Jews can foreshorten his coming in performing the *mitsva* of *aliyah*—the religious obligation to "go up" to *erets*—and so precede the messiah as to welcome him there.

Here we have no compensating ideologies or transposition of rituals, but rather an immediate decision. *Aliyah* alone can effectively initiate the messianic redemption, by an immense act of faith in the mystical power of *erets.* And so we have the *olim,* the unending procession of those who, in a capital moment in their lives, have decided to "orient" not only their prayers, their offerings, and their hopes, but the final concrete reality of their existence. Certain ones among them—Juda Halevi, Yehiel of Paris, Nachmanides, Moshe Hayim Luzzato—gave a meaning to their experience of *aliyah* which would nourish, guide, and illumine the generations to come, "going up" from *Hibbat Zion* or from Zionist motives.

Sometimes the motivation is cultural—part political, part spiritual. For Yehiel or Nachmanides, it was a matter of building the *yishuv,* establishing a concrete community of Jews in *erets* in an effort to incarnate the solidarity between *erets* and the people of Israel. At other times the reasons are purely political, but in the Jewish perspective of messianic politics which is identified with a spiritual goal. Such was the case with Sabbatai Zvi, who was not the only one to dream of a messianic kingdom in *erets.* On a more realistic level, the famous exegete of the Mishna, Obadya Bartenra, noted after his *aliyah* to *erets* in the fifteenth century: "Oh, with but one person expert in matters political we could peacefully establish ourselves in Palestine and inaugurate the Jewish kingdom!" Still again, one may be moved by a vague but irresistible impulse, a call to leave behind tranquillity and one's home—Juda Halevi, the twelfth century Spanish exile, and Luzzato from eighteenth century Amsterdam—to encounter storms and shoals, if only to die in the prime of life at the very moment of arrival in *erets!* No matter; for what would otherwise be an absurd tragedy here becomes an experience to unify all others: the mystical attainment of the absolute.

There is something of this absolute in Zionism and its achievement, the state of Israel, which can be regarded as the fruit of the land of Israel. For it is only in *Erets Israel* that the Zionist state is faithful to its Jewish identity, to its messianic vocation, and to the name which it took: identical with that of the land on which it is built—the state of *Israel.*

If one could indicate a date in the history of Zionism which would illustrate how the land of Israel became the irreplaceable support for a Jewish state, none would be more decisive than the 23rd of August 1903, at the sixth Zionist congress in Basle—the last congress in which Theodor Herzl participated.

In 1903 many Jews had immigrated to western Europe from Russia in the wake of the frightful pogroms. The British government offered Herzl a place to receive them: the territory of Uganda in central East Africa. Herzl was inclined to accept this proposition and inaugurate a Jewish home on African soil. It was the delegates from Russia, however, immediately affected by the pogroms, who valiantly recalled the "Zionist" dimension of Zionism, threatening to withdraw their own militants from Herzl's movement if he persisted in betraying the holy land for the sake of another territory. The Russian delegates fought for an entire night *against* the Uganda proposal, in favor of the "Zionism of Zion," of Palestine-*Erets Israel.*

In a few lines which cannot be read without emotion, Herzl alludes to the sixth congress in his *Journal* of August 31, 1903, where he acknowledges the experience to have been difficult yet splendid. Not realizing that this was to be his last, Herzl imagines the speech he will make to the seventh congress ". . . if it is granted to me to live. By that time, either I will have Palestine, or I will have become convinced of the utter absurdity in continuing to work for that goal. If the latter be the case, I will simply have to say that it is impossible. Our goal has not been reached, nor will it be in a foreseeable future. Yet we have a partial achievement: this other territory (Uganda) where we could locate those of our people who are needy, and do so on a national footing with an autonomous administration. I do not believe we have the right to deny these unfortunate people some relief for reasons of legitimacy or in the name of a beautiful dream. Yet I realize full well that our movement is rent by a decisive schism, and that the division cuts right through me. Although originally I was only in favor of a Jewish state—wherever it might be located—later I too took up the banner of Zion, and became a lover of Zion. Palestine is the only country where our people could find a resting place, but, meanwhile, hundreds of thousands of people need immediate help. The only way to resolve this dilemma is for me to give up the direction of the movement. Henceforth we should have two action committees: one for East Africa, the other for Palestine. I would not belong to either one. . . ."

These reflections are replete with too many alternatives, dilemmas—too many "buts." The absolute did not permit Herzl to vacillate. Herzl would die before having to give this speech, and his final directives to the Zionist movement would not be this perspective of the "two ways" but the totality of his life and prophetic thought which would direct Zionism toward its sole authentic objective: Zion. Everything worked out as though fate wanted to keep Herzl from having to choose somewhere else at the moment when the notion of the land presented itself to him in the full force of its mystical significance. For this land gives one no choice but to make a total offering of one's self—willing or not.

IV
THE LAND OF ISRAEL:
WHERE CONTRADICTIONS ARE OVERCOME

The state of Israel, then, has given itself to this land. No other territory could give birth to a Jewish state. Concrete attempts had been made: in Argentina in the nineteenth century, by Soviet Russia in the twentieth, in Birobidjan in Siberia. They all failed. Only the state of Israel succeeded, showing an undeniable faith in its tenure, on the land. Yet this faith reflects the fact that, for a Jew, to choose or to renounce the word Zion is a solemn act: it amounts to overcoming apparently irreconcilable contradictions. And the Zionist movement, together with its consummation—the state of Israel—has given its consent to this act, choosing, along with the biblical land, the paradoxes of the biblical vocation.

A paradox first of language. During the exile, Jews had adopted for their common speech either the language of the countries themselves, or dialects amalgamating local elements with a Hebrew base—Yiddish or Ladino. Hebrew remained nearly exclusively the language of liturgy or of learning. Yet, refusing the temptation of modern languages—Herzl had thought at the outset of German—the Zionists chose Hebrew as the national language, respecting its biblical roots, yet making it into a complete and dynamic tool of contemporary expression.

The paradox of culture: The individual and the collective, the particular and universal, the sacred and profane, are interwoven in the Bible in a complex yet irreducible dialectic. Zionism has not hesitated in the face of any of these difficulties, confronting them with a sense of faithfully serving its biblical vocation.

Paradox finally of its situation: Is not the Bible the place where the three monotheistic religions both meet and diverge? Will not the choice of the biblical land concretize on the terrain itself this paradoxical intersection? Nevertheless Zionism and the state it created situate themselves here in full awareness.

All of these factors which increase and aggravate the problems of the state at once accentuate its isolation and its responsibilities as well. Relations with the rest of the world become difficult and often intractable, the question of "holy places" inescapably arises, yet kibbutzim can be established; real estate speculation is tempered by levitical legislation, yet private initiative is encouraged in those domains where the Bible has not legislated. In sum, all this complicates a mode of life which nevertheless, by the very fact of this complexity, is alone worthy to bear the name it has chosen for itself: *Israel*. It is this immense tension which Israelis carry in their hearts—and not merely a pioneering pride or an atavism of the land and its dead—when they say: Palestine is our land. Or when they say *"Erets Israel"* and when they create on this land the state of Israel.

In the book of Exodus, before promulgating the ten commandments, God announces to the Jewish people:

> If only you will now listen to me and keep my covenant, then out of all peoples you shall become my special possession, for the whole earth is mine. You shall be my kingdom of priests, my holy nation (19:5).

The *segulah*, the election of Israel, is an election to responsibility—to a transforming responsibility whose purpose is to accept whatever comes along in its train. For Israel did not merely accept not to kill, but to go much further: to transform sword into ploughshare, to make murder impossible. Israel did not simply accept not to commit adultery or debauchery, but to transmute passion into conjugal love and to make debauchery impossible because it would become love. Israel did not merely receive the land of Canaan (a name preserved in the Bible), but took on as well the vocation to transform that land into the land of Israel.

Here we touch on the conditional theme in creation. In the Jewish conception, God did not, in creating the world, give it a pre-set orientation which would make it move necessarily toward its goal from the outset. God created the world *on condition,* at the risk of a radical insecurity. The talmudic Midrash has God saying—after destroying twenty-six worlds, none of which satisfied him, and having just created ours, the twenty-seventh: "Provided it holds!" God himself could not guarantee the world would hold, because it would only do so if human beings would play their part. As Abraham Heschel so aptly put it: "God needs man." God did not create the world for it to follow automatically a divine plan. Creation is a risk God took, and humankind is to share in the risk. The Jewish people took on this risk in full responsibility. Accordingly, the risk will be extended to the promised kingdom of priests (*mamlekheth kohanim*), a holy people (*goy kadosh*)—a *people* in the most concrete and physical sense of that term, a *kingdom* in the sense that word has in the Bible and which we render today as "state." The Jewish people took on the land of Israel, with all its paradoxes, to realize its central and messianic character, and to take on an additional risk as well: the creation of a state.

It is the greatness as well as the risk of Zionism to have introduced a political element, the creation of a state, into a scale of values already difficult to reconcile among themselves: survival and ethical demands, collectivity and the need for individuality. The dreadful additional burden, not only accepted but required of the Jewish people after Auschwitz, is to reconcile the state with messianic demands. That means, in the words of Martin Buber, to want to establish *utopia* on the *topos* (space), to establish utopia on the land—to give a *topos* (place) to *utopia* (no-place). And such a task can be realized only by reconciling three primordial irreconcilable facts.

(a) First reconciliation: to make an ensemble of peoples, especially the peoples of the Bible.

Jerusalem especially provokes conflict among Jews, Christians, and Muslims. It is an unavoidable conflict, for love for the holy places among Christians and Muslims reflects genuine devotion. Judaism regards its intention to gather the people to the land and create the state of Israel to imply, among other tasks, the reconciliation of these three irreconcilables: an encounter among the three peoples of the Bible, and of all humankind across our multiple divisions. The state of Israel is delighted and proud of the fact that it is only since June 1967 that one may hear the same morning in Jerusalem: bells calling Christians to church, the muezzin calling the Muslims to prayer, and the blast of a shofar inviting Jews to pray. This is certainly one of the startling results of the reunification of the city, and it marks a first in the history of Jerusalem.

For when the Jews originally held sway over Jerusalem neither Christianity nor Islam yet existed. During the historical epoch in which Christianity developed, Jews were ever subdued and humbled in Jerusalem. And when Islam arose, it oppressed in turn the two biblical religions which preceded it. Not during the crusades, nor under Islamic rule, nor even under the British mandate (except for the short period from 1920 to 1929) did Jews enjoy entirely free access to their holy places.

Judah Halevi in the high middle ages saw a sign of Jewish election for Israel and for the state in the love which so many peoples—peoples of antiquity, Christians and Muslims—held for Jerusalem. "How can we fail to be certain that our people have been chosen to gather into one on this land when we have before us the tangible sign of the love which others bear for this land—a love so faithful that they seek after it, ponder over it, and pray for it . . . ?" (*Kuzari* II, 20). Since 1967 the state of Israel has been trying to bring together in mutual understanding, work and prayer those same peoples who at one time fought among themselves, sword in hand, for the prize of Jerusalem.

(b) Second reconciliation: sacred and profane.

Assimilated Jews as well as Marxists, socialists, communists and atheists all collaborated, together with religious Jews and Jewish believers, to promote the state. Is the state of Israel a religious or a secular state? It is both at once, sacred and profane in an inextricable fashion, and this makes it a Jewish state. If it had been created as a purely religious (or "clerical") state, it would not be a Jewish state; if it had been established as a thoroughgoing Marxist state, it would not have been Jewish either. It is a Jewish state because it is both. The state of Israel offers an exemplar of the co-existence of atheism and belief as well as their daily collaboration on every level.

(c) Third reconciliation—within the Jewish people—between "patient" and "impatient" messianic hopes.

Some Jews see the first signs of messianic deliverance in the very existence of the state of Israel. Others insist: "Not yet!" Not satisfied with the dawning on earth of a return to the land, they await a sign from on high, a miracle from heaven. But patience cohabits with impatience in the state of Israel. Today these two contradictory tendencies crystallize politically in various spectra. But patient and impatient are branches of one and the same Jewish people. They would sketch different paths, yet the route is the same—that of the state of Israel, traced out among all the novel and unforeseen possibilities the twentieth century has to offer, on the irreplaceable land of the Jewish people.

[Translated from French by David Burrell, C.S.C. with assistance from Paul Burrell]

The Sacred Character of the Land

Shahé Ajamian

In addressing the subject of sacred geography, I am referring to that portion of the earthly globe which surrounds Mount Ararat. The Bible tells us: "And in the seventh month, on the seventeenth day of the month, the ark came to rest upon the mountains of Ararat" (Gen 8:4). This was the same mountain of Ararat which remains, to this day, the focal point of so many stories and popular legends. One such legend has it that the animals in Noah's ark could speak, especially the birds. When Noah released the dove to carry out the mission which the raven had failed to accomplish, the raven flew at the dove and bit off its tongue. The dove was consequently unable to describe what it had seen and that is why it brought the symbolic olive branch to Noah, plucked from the land around Ararat after the flood waters had subsided.

According to the Bible, the patriarch then emerged from the ark together with his sons, their wives, and all the animals, one species after the other. Noah's first act was to build an altar to God and sacrifice beasts and fowl there. The Bible goes on to recount that God, having "smelled the pleasing odor" of the burnt offerings, promised: "I will never again curse the ground because of man, for the imagination of man's heart is evil from his youth; neither will I ever again destroy every living creature as I have done. While the earth remains, seedtime and harvest, cold and heat, summer and winter, day and night, shall not cease" (Gen 8:20–22).

The precise spot where God smelled the pleasing odor of the burnt offerings at the first altar erected in worshipful gratitude by Noah was, according to Armenian tradition, on the hillock facing Mount Ararat now occupied by the Monastery of Khor Virab, the "deep dungeon." The land never again to be cursed is, geographically, the land of Armenia.

30

If one stands today on the recently reconstructed ramparts of this monastery and surveys the majestic mountain, its summit seems tiny and quite near. In fact, this mass of rock is over 16,500 feet high. With a slight stretch of the imagination, one can easily conjure up the scene when Noah, his children and all the animals in the ark came ashore at this very spot. You can almost see the familiar figures coming toward you, led by the righteous patriarch. It is not hard to understand how the story of the flood and Noah's ark have retained their vividness in the minds of the people in this part of the world.

As it happens, this is also the site of another overwhelming event in the history of the Armenian nation, that of the "deep dungeon." At the end of the third century, this monastery was the fortress of the capital of the Armenian kingdom, Artachad, which was established by Artaxerxes. Gregory the Christian, scribe of King Tiridates III, had survived all the tortures inflicted on him by those who wanted to avenge the assassination of Archak, father of Tiridates, who was treacherously murdered by Gregory's father, Anak, while they were out hunting. Gregory was thrown into the fortress dungeon for refusing to deny his faith. And from this dungeon of death emerged the holy man, after thirteen years of oblivion, in order to convert Armenia to Christianity in the year 301.

This miraculous survival by the messenger, whom God sent to attach the Armenian people to him, occurred at the same spot where Noah built his altar. The cupola of the Monastery of Khor Virab rises above the hilltop facing Ararat where, from the time of St. John of Nisibis until today, men have gone in search of a piece of wood from the ark, that tiny rise buried under eternal snow which popular belief still takes for Noah's ark.

The history of Armenia comprises three thousand years of struggle against invaders who, like floods, often engulfed the local population in a blood bath. The ark on its sacred mountain and the cupola of the Khor Virab are symbols of the miraculous survival of the Armenian people on their own land. The conversion to Christianity was seen as the return of the nation, by means of an everlasting covenant, to the God of Noah, the "just man, perfect in his generations" (Gen 6:9), father of the world and lord of the earth.

The creed of the survival of this people in its native land is described by a fourth century historian named Faustus Byzantinus. In the twelfth chapter of his *History of Armenia,* he recounts the story of Archak II, the Armenian monarch who for thirty years fought against the Byzantines on the one hand and the Persians on the other. Archak is invited for peace negotiations by Shapur, the Persian king. But at the banquet which precedes the talks, Shapur has his guest arrested on the pretext that Archak refused to be converted to fire worship. The peace parley, however, takes place and the king of Persia is eventually satisfied that a military pact against Byzantium is feasible. At this point Persian priests intervene to warn their king that an Armenian king is not to be trusted if he is not standing on his native soil.

> So then King Shapur ordered half the ground before the altar to be covered with earth and water brought from Armenia, while the other half would remain unchanged. He summoned Archak, king of the Armenians, and dismissed everyone else from his presence. Taking Archak's arm, he began to stroll about. When he stood in front of the altar, on Persian ground, he said: "O Archak, king of the Armenians, why have you become my enemy? I who loved you as my son, who had hoped to give you my daughter in marriage so that you would be my son as you gave your word. But you, of your own free will and not through mine, you have turned into my foe and have been waging war against me these thirty years." To which Archak replied: "I have sinned against you by coming here; when I killed or drove off your enemies, I expected you to reward me but your enemies won me over; I feared you and ran away. It was only my vow to you which made me return. Now here I am, your servant; do with me whatever you please. Kill me. I am in your hands. I your servant have sinned against you and deserve to die." But Shapur, taking his arm again, steered him toward the area covered by the earth of Armenia. As soon as Archak stepped on his native soil, he regained his assurance; his tone changed and he spoke with confident pride: "Keep your distance from me, vile servant who has made himself master. In the name of my ancestors, I intend to take revenge on you and your sons for the murder of King Ardavan." Once back on Persian soil, Archak regretted his impulse and his impertinent words. But no sooner were the two men on Armenian soil again than Archak expressed himself even more harshly. As the day wore on, Shapur tempted his adversary a number of times, and whereas Archak had the upper hand on Armenian ground, when on Persian ground he fell on his knees and begged forgiveness.

As we see from this passage, it is a well established tradition that the land, consisting of "dust and water," inspires courage and strengthens the king, himself the personification of the people. The bond between land and king is a physical one, the very existence of the people on that land. It is a bond of strength, for a nation feels strong when it irrigates its own land with water from its own river.

Following the First World War, the exiled survivors of the Armenian massacres were faced with a dilemma: Could they consider the Soviet Republic of Armenia, that ray of hope envisaged by the martyrs, as the fulfillment of a grand dream, the motherland reborn? Some, unable to tolerate the regime, tried to create an abstract patriotism which put forward the idea of a "spiritual Armenia" based on a sense of identity, on preserving the national heritage, the language, traditions and, above all, the enduring dream of a united and independent country. This was the Armenia of the exiles in the diaspora without a hearth, without a land. Every Armenian today is as aware as his former king was of the very real force of his identity, whenever he treads on the native soil of his ancestors.

There are various possible explanations for this phenomenon. The first Armenian historian, Moses of Chorene who lived in the fifth century, offered a biblical interpretation according to which the three sons of Noah are the forefathers of the entire human race. Shem is the ancestor of Abraham; Ham is the ancestor of the Babylonians, the people of Mesopotamia, Egypt and Ethiopia; Japhet is the ancestor of the Armenians. The same historian traced the origins of the royal families of Armenia. He discovered that the house of Bagratid has as ancestor "one of the princes of the Hebrews, brought by Nebuchadnezzar as a slave, and named Shambath. . . ." This historian attempted to draw a parallel between Abraham's settling in Canaan and the ancestor of the Armenians in Armenia. However, he did not explicitly mention the concept of the covenant, presenting instead a different idea: the strength to defend one's land is God-given. The inspiration behind the courageous deeds in Armenian epic history stems from the well-known principle expressed by Chorene: "The frontiers of the brave reside in his sword; he possesses what he cuts." If God has promised you a portion of land, he will give you the strength to defend it.

The Armenian word for "promise," when it refers to land, is "annunciated lands" in the sense of the annunciation, implying that what is unthinkable or impossible for man is indeed possible for God. It is God who promised and who announces the realization of his promise. The conclusion to be drawn is that only in a promised land of this nature can a people become a *nation*.

In the year 301, Saint Gregory the Illuminator emerged from the "deep dungeon," baptized the king, the court and all the people and experienced a vision. He saw Christ descending toward the land of Ararat, tapping a specific place with a golden hammer and tracing in lines of light the outline of the cathedral of the Armenian Church. Christ's voice spoke to Gregory: "Here you will build my church. . . ." The name of the church remains, to this day, *Etchmiadzine* or "The Descent of the First-Born" (Jesus). It is the temple, or Vatican, of the Armenians.

One hundred years later, another vision disclosed the alphabet as commemorated in the Armenian national anthem: "Like Moses, Vartabed our Lord, Thou hast brought the text of the law to the Armenian world and hast enlightened the generations which followed after Torkom and his sons."

These few lines of the anthem, dedicated to Saint Mesrob, inventor of the Armenian alphabet, amply illustrate Armenian history in terms of the Christianization of Armenia. In the same way that Moses brought the law to the people in the desert, St. Mesrob brought the alphabet to the people of the mountains. He set out, in fact, to discover the alphabet with the clearly defined purpose of translating the Bible. And, like Moses, the holy translator of the Bible discovered the alphabet in a vision: "Not in a dream while asleep, and not awake, but through the eyes of his heart, he saw" the right hand of the Lord drawing the characters of the Armenian alphabet in luminous lines through the darkness of his monastic cell. This is the alphabet which transmitted the light of divine law to the "sons of Torkom." Torkom is the Armenian equivalent for the name Togarmah, son of Gomer, son of Japhet, ancestor of "Beth-togarmah: from the uttermost parts of the north" (Ez 38:6).

These two visions endowed the people of Ararat with the temple and the language, the two poles of a national culture. Thus the three constituent elements of a national church were established, land, faith and culture, all three conceived in the divine perspective. The land was where Christ came down on earth; the faith was the new covenant which bound the people of Beth-togarmah to the God of Noah; the culture was initiated by an eternal light.

Armenians consider it a privilege, accorded by God, to have been the first to be baptized as a nation. The waters of the flood had purified the earth at the spot where Noah and his sons descended from the ark. Similarly, the waters of the River Araxe, where the king and his court were baptized by St. Gregory, sanctified and purified the Armenian people. As the Spirit hovered above the waters before descending over the Jordan, so the holy chrism (*muron*) is sprinkled on the head of the baptized, who is anointed by the Spirit as he or she emerges from the baptismal immersion.

The Christianization of Armenia thus signified the return of an entire people to the worship of God, forgotten by the descendants of Noah. It was the renewal of the eternal covenant with the patriarch which found new expression in the holy oil with which the baptized is anointed on every part of his body. The Armenian word for baptism is *genounk* which literally means consecration or seal. When the priest applies the holy ointment to the forehead, he says: "Sweet oil, in the name of Jesus Christ, seal of the heavenly gifts of immortality. . . ." The Book of Sacraments stipulates that a newborn infant must be brought to the church on its eighth day. Basil of Caesarea (Basil the Great) canonized this custom: "Let the newly born child not be kept for more than six or seven days without the seal (of baptism). . . ." This canon entered Armenian canon law as soon as it was introduced in the fourth century.

The epistle of Makarios, patriarch of Jerusalem, addressed in the 330s to Verdanes, St. Gregory's son and successor, mentions two kinds of holy oil used in the dispensation of the sacraments: "I bequeath to you these canons which I learned from the stories of the apostles and which the tradition of the fathers has firmly established among us. As I have mentioned before, the sanction of the holy christening must be performed by the bishops or priests. And the holy oil must be blessed by the head of the bishops (the archbishop or, rather, the catholicos). As for the anointing oil for the sick, the deceased. . . ."

The holy oil, the chrism or *muron,* is to this day consecrated by the catholicos assisted by twelve bishops in a magnificent ceremony. The holy oil is prepared forty days in advance, using olive and balsam for the base. The Book of Sacraments recommends Jerusalem balsam, perfumed with flowers and specific roots mentioned in the ritual. On the day of consecration of the holy oil, the catholicos pours old oil into the new and mixes it with the relics of St. Gregory's right hand, as a sign of continuity. It continues the descent of the Holy Ghost over the Jordan on the day when Jesus Christ was baptized, and the hymn sung on this occasion is addressed to the Spirit of God, reflecting the words of Isaiah: "The Spirit of the Lord God is upon me because the Lord has anointed me" (61:1).

The entire ritual of the sacraments of the Armenian Church is based on the idea of heritage, the inheritance of the pact between God and his people. "And I will take you for my people, and I will be your God" (Ex 6:7). Moses said to God: "Take us for your inheritance." And the Lord said, "Behold I make a covenant" (Ex 34:9–10). The hymn sung at every christening celebrates this with the words: "In Christ we are called the new Israel: We have become the inheritance of the Lord and the co-inheritors of Christ." This is a reference to the passage in Galatians 3:29: "If you are Christ's, then you are Abraham's offspring, heirs according to promise." And further, in 4:4–7: "But when the time had fully come, God sent forth his Son, born of woman, born under the law, to redeem those who were under the law, so that we might receive adoption as sons. And because you are sons, God has sent the spirit of his Son into our hearts, crying 'Abba! Father!' So through God you are no longer a slave but a son, and if a son then an heir."

This is precisely how an Armenian sees the christening ceremony: the descent of the Spirit sent by the Father through the Son, in order to render the newborn child a son of Abraham, an heir to the first covenant between God and his people and, through the blood of the Son, an heir to the new covenant *by adoption,* having become the son of Abraham. This is why immediately after the christening, the infant receives communion since, according to the exact words of the immersion rite, the baptized "servant of the Lord (name) . . . accepts adoption by the Heavenly Father, in order to become co-heir of Christ and the Temple of the Holy Spirit." Thanks to this adoption, the child thus becomes a member of the great house of God, the church, a member of the "people of God," the "new Israel" with whom the covenant—the New Testament—is sealed by the blood spilt on the cross. The mark of this new title of "son of Abraham, heir to the first covenant" is the holy chrism. "And God said to Abraham, 'As for you, you shall keep my covenant, you and your descendants after you through-out their generations. This is my covenant, which you shall keep . . . so shall my covenant be in your flesh an everlasting covenant' " (Gen 17:9–13).

These words, in their accepted Christian connotation, still retain—in their ritual symbolism as in their theological significance—the profound concept of salvation contained in the Old Testament, in which God makes a covenant with an entire nation. In order to mark the covenant "in the flesh," the baptized infant is anointed all over when he comes out of the ritual water: on his forehead, his eyes, his ears, his nose, his mouth, his hands, his feet, his chest, and his back. He is anointed by the *muron,* the holy chrism, "seal of the incorruptible gifts of heaven."

The purpose of the covenant was to make the nation into "a chosen race, a royal priesthood, a holy nation, God's own people" (1 Pet 2:9), in the image of the covenant of Sinai where the message transmitted to Moses said: "If you will obey my voice and keep my covenant, then you shall be a peculiar treasure unto me above all people: for all the earth is mine. You shall be unto me a kingdom of priests, and a holy nation" (Ex 19:5–6).

In order to become a kingdom of priests worshiping the Lord, every one of the children of Israel had to be "ransomed (redeemed), purified and consecrated," in the Christian reinterpretation, by "the precious blood of Christ, as of a lamb without blemish and without spot" (1 Pet 1:19), purified by the baptismal waters and consecrated by the holy ointment or chrism.

The founder of the Armenian Church, St. Gregory, describes this conversion as follows: "In place of the haughty tower, soon in ruins, the cross of truth has been ensconced, whose power is eternal and whose glory is the Lord." He quotes the prophet Isaiah: "The Lord shall arise upon you and his glory shall be seen upon you. Nations shall come to your light, and kings to the brightness of your rising" (Is 60:2–3).

God wanted the "sons of Togarmah" to have the privilege of leading this march of nations toward the light and the rising brightness of faith. This was thanks to the great saint, glorified in the Armenian hymn: "The holy Pontiff, Preacher of the True Word of God, presented a new nation to the Lord, purified of its sins and invited to the glory of the heights of Zion." The "heights of Zion," both figuratively and actually, were the inheritance of this nation from the earliest centuries in the history of the Christian church in Jerusalem. From the fourth century onward, Armenian monks and bishops came to retire and live out their lives of meditation or pilgrimage in the monasteries of Jerusalem and the Judean desert. Beckoned to the heights of Zion, throngs of pilgrims swept down from the heights of Armenia or set sail from Cilician ports on their way to pray and to listen as they heeded the call of Isaiah: "Come and let us go up to the mountain of the Lord, to the house of the God of Jacob, and he will teach us of his ways" (2:3).

The church in Jerusalem became the school where the canon law of prayer, the *lex orandi,* was elaborated, its ritual and lectionary following the Judaic traditions of the Judeo-Christian community. From the beginning, it was adopted by the Armenians who worked on it, adapting it to their own requirements but basically preserving it until today. Nowadays, the Armenian monastery of St. James in Jerusalem is the only one where the daily prayers are still recited in entirety, beginning with the reading of the psalms before daybreak and continuing until the hour of rest, at nightfall.

The festivals of the Christian year here in Jerusalem maintain gestures and popular traditions inherited from Jewish customs, "for my house shall be called a house of prayer for all peoples" (Is 56:7). In this conservatism regarding traditions born in Jerusalem, the overriding feeling is of an unbroken line ever since the time when King Solomon dedicated the temple and reminded God of his promise, "that my name might be therein" (1 Kgs 8:16), although Solomon wondered whether "God will indeed dwell on the earth?" (v. 27). This is the continuity of the benediction received by "those who have confidence in the Lord" and who glorify him, as in Psalm 147 which begins with the doxology: "Praise the Lord, O Jerusalem, praise your God, O Zion. For he has strengthened the bars of your gates; he has blessed your children within you" (vv. 12–13).

For succeeding generations of Armenians who have come on pilgrimage to Jerusalem, have chosen to live there, have built their cathedral on Mount Zion or have desired to end their days in Jerusalem in order to enjoy the great privilege of being interred on Mount Zion—for all these, Jerusalem is not merely a city where one lives a comfortable life, nor a splendid capital synonymous with prestige, inscribed in golden letters on a map. Jerusalem is much more: a symbol, a promise, an entire theology, a hymn to the glory of God. Loved by believers, Jerusalem will always be the object of covetousness and the source of disputes.

What distinguishes this city from all others is its situation, chosen for no strategic, economic or political consideration. For the selection of this city to become "a house of prayer for all peoples" is a divine choice. Atop mountains at the edge of the desolate Judean desert, barely provided with water and far from the main trading routes, Jerusalem possesses none of the qualities essential for a flourishing capital city. All the same, when God wanted to communicate with his people, as he had spoken to Moses at Sinai, it was in Jerusalem that he chose to proclaim his name and to demand that "three times in the year all your males shall appear before the Lord God" (Ex 23:17) to celebrate the three pilgrimage festivals and bring the "first-fruits of your land" into the house of the Lord (v. 19).

For those who received the law of love as the supreme utterance and definitive message of the gospel, promulgated by their savior from the heights of Zion at the last supper, this is surely the fulfillment of Isaiah's prophecy: "For out of Zion shall go forth the law and the word of the Lord from Jerusalem" (2:3).

And for the generations to come, the name of Jerusalem will remain sanctified by a history written by a divine hand, the history of God on earth. We will repeat Jacob's words: "How dreadful is this place! This is none other but the house of God, and this is the gate of heaven" (Gen 28:17).

Israel and Jewish Self-Understanding

Pinchas Hacohen Peli

On the seventeenth of Kislev, 5708 (November 29, 1947), the United
Nations voted by a majority of more than two-thirds to partition the land
of Israel, which was then under the British Mandate, and to establish a
Jewish state. That decision was preceded by the Balfour Declaration of
1917 and the decision of the League of Nations at the San Remo Conference in 1921 promising to fulfill the aspirations of the Zionist movement
for the return of the Jewish people to independent life in its homeland.

On the fifth of Iyyar, 5708 (May 14, 1948) the state of Israel was
established. Today it is a national, geopolitical, and military entity, and as
such is a member of the United Nations, recognized by most of the nations of the world—both by those which, to some degree, view it favorably
and value its achievements and what it represents, and also by those which
accept it with indifference as one nation among the others. And Israel
perceives itself as a nation among the others.

Whatever the nuances of the ongoing ideological and semantic debate, the fact remains that the Jews are a nation as well as a religious
community. We do not know of Jews who do not belong to Judaism. As
long as they have not assumed another faith, even if they do not observe
the commandments of the Jewish religion, they are Jews. From the moment they convert to another religion they are no longer Jews, and they
have left the Jewish people. Similarly, people who accept Judaism do not
merely accept the principles of the Jewish faith but they also become Jews,
members of the Jewish people and part of Jewish history.

The separation of Judaism as a religion from Jewish history is incon-
ceivable. From its beginnings, faith and history have been bound together
in Judaism. The Bible, God's will as revealed to humanity, is mainly

39

concerned with history—first, with that of the patriarchs, for whose purpose the history of the world is told, and afterward the story of everything
that happened to the Jewish people. The history of that people—the fortunate and the tragic events—is Torah, divine teaching. As early as the
period of the judges, before there was a king in Israel, the Bible tells of
Ruth the Moabite who comes and accepts the God of Israel. When she
addresses her mother-in-law, Naomi, she does not merely say, "Your God
is my God," but first she says, "Your people shall be my people"; for to be
a Jew means to accept the God of Israel, but also the people of Israel, to be
part of it and to share its fate: "Where you die, I will die" (Ru 1:17). More
than two thousand years later, in the thirteenth century, when Ovadia the
convert addressed the greatest rabbi of the generation, Moses Maimonides, asking him how it can be that someone whose ancestors were idolators in the Arabian desert can sincerely say in his prayers, "Our God and
God of our fathers, the God of Abraham, the God of Isaac, and the God of
Jacob" (for he alone became a Jew, whereas his ancestors were idolators),
Maimonides answered him with a well known responsum: this convert is
right in calling the fathers of the Hebrew nation his fathers, for from the
moment that he accepted Judaism, he also took Jewish history upon himself, not only its future, but also its past and present.

The Bible is not a book of theology, that is, of concepts about God,
but is rather a compendium of anthropology and history from the point of
view of God. The reality of history, the existence of the Jewish state today,
necessarily confronts us with the following question: What is the meaning
of this state in the eyes of God? In other words, what is the religious meaning of this most recent bit of history, according to the self-
understanding of Judaism as an integration of faith and history?

We can not avoid posing this question. Just as Judaism does not exist
outside of history, history for the Jew does not exist outside of Judaism
and its basic values. History cannot be indifferent or meaningless, for the
Jew is commanded to "understand the years of each generation" and to
learn lessons from historical events. That is the case in the Bible and in
rabbinical literature, as well as in later philosophical and moral writings.
Even today history is not indifferent, and it has meaning. The major
difference between our era and the earlier generations is that we do not
have, as they did, prophets or Urim and Thummim[1] to interpret events.
Nevertheless, just as that lack has not prevented Judaism from developing
a creative and active life in all areas of religious law, legend, thought and
ethics, similarly there is definitely the possibility, even the religious obliga-

tion, to attempt to discern the meaning within contemporary historical events.

During the past thirty years, extensive religious literature has been written attempting to clarify the religious status of the state of Israel, which appears, from its visible characteristics to be merely a political and military, i.e. a secular, entity. We said "visible characteristics" because many people assess Israeli life by more intrinsic critera. I am not referring now to the small minority which wishes to see Israel as a biblical, theocratic Jewish state. Of more relevance and significance is the faith-perception of those Jews who experience Israel as a stage in messianic redemption, the expectation of which is one of the central elements in Judaism. This messianism is interwoven through all Jewish literature and prayers, and is counted as one of Maimonides' Thirteen Principles of Faith (in fact, the final, conclusive tenet), the credo accepted in every Jewish household for centuries.

Although belief in the coming of the messiah became a basic foundation of the Jewish religion very early, from the start there have been two different views with regard to the actual meaning of that belief. In the first centuries of the common era, the rabbinic sages were divided as to whether it was an eschatological and apocalyptical messianism which would completely reverse the natural laws of the cosmos, or whether it was a realistic event or series of events which would occur within history. Both those views were based on the visions of the prophets and on the paradigm of the first redemption, the exodus from Egypt.

"Normative" Jewish thought has taken after those Talmudic sages who sought to differentiate between apocalyptic and realistic conceptions. For example, Rabbi Hiyya Bar Abba said in the name of Rabbi Yohanan: All of the prophets prophesied only about the days of the messiah, but as for the world to come, "No eye has yet seen it."[2] In general, Jewish thought adopts the view of Samuel in the Talmud,[3] which is also adopted by Maimonides in his masterpiece of religious laws, the *Mishneh Torah,* "The only difference between this era and the messianic age lies in deliverance from subjection to alien rulers."[4] But hopes for messianic redemption have not been limited to the desire for political independence, as it might appear from that formulation. Maimonides warns against erroneous thinking concerning changes in the laws of nature in the messianic age: "Do not think that the messianic king must perform signs and wonders, create new things in this world, revive the dead, or things of that sort. That is not the case."[5] However, he does link the messianic age with the fulfillment of other hopes, such as the reconstruction of the Temple, the ingathering of the exiles, and the restoration of the Davidic monarchy under a righteous king, "who meditates on the Torah and performs its commandments like his ancestor David, as prescribed in both the Written and the Oral Torah, and prevails upon all Jews to walk in the way of the Torah. . . ."[6]

Even if one holds that on the fifth of Iyyar, 5708, with the establishment of the Jewish state, servitude to foreign nations ceased (an opinion which must be examined and clarified), we cannot on that basis alone determine the religious status of the state. If we take the traditional belief about the future redemption and the messianic age as a yardstick, we must still consider what other signs and indications identify the messianic age, and whether they are actually manifested in the present-day state of Israel.

So the question which tradition and history pose is: Does the state of Israel belong to the time frame of the messianic age, and, if so, to what extent? The examination of that question entails the clarification of other issues, such as the nature of miracles and trials, the nature of exile and redemption, the signs of the end of exile and the beginnings of redemption, the chronological and theological propinquity of the Holocaust and the establishment of the state, none of which are simple matters. For example, someone who holds that the establishment of the state and its military victories are of a miraculous nature must still seek the religious significance of those miracles, which do not in themselves, according to the Jewish view, answer the essential religious question for which they are invoked as evidence. In the dramatic confrontation between the prophet Elijah and the prophets of Baal on Mount Carmel, at the critical moment after he had finished his preparations for the trial, Elijah prays to God, saying: "Answer me, O Lord, answer me, and let this people know that thou, Lord, art God and that it is thou that hast caused them to be backsliders" (1 Kgs 18:37). Why, ask the rabbis, does Elijah repeat himself, "Answer me . . . answer me"? Their answer is: "Answer me and make fire come down from the heavens, and answer me so that they do not say that it was an act of sorcery."[7] Fire descending from heaven is not enough in itself, for that which one person considers to be a manifest miracle can be considered by someone else as an act of sorcery or as a trial to test man. If in fact, as many people think, miracles occurred with the establishment of the state of Israel (and some have listed them—a very impressive list), what can those miracles mean to us, the generation after Auschwitz and

Treblinka, a generation without a visionary or a prophet, a generation for whom the gates of heaven are sealed?

Seemingly we are up a blind alley, and there is no one among us who can testify as to the meaning of these most recent historical events. But, in fact, that is not the case. Almost all the thinkers who have dealt with this subject have refused to leave the question unresolved, and each of them has sought a solution according to his own inclinations and method. We can distinguish their arguments according to the following typology of approaches to this subject: a prophetic approach; a midrashic approach; a halakhic approach. Each of these categories can be further subdivided into negative and positive attitudes, as we shall elaborate.

The "positive prophetic approach" includes all those who believe, beyond any doubt, that the events of our day definitely possess a messianic dimension. Some of them disagree concerning the extent of that dimension, that is, whether we are in an advanced stage of messianic redemption or simply in its earlier manifestations, *athalta de-geula,* in Aramaic, the beginning of redemption. Yet all of them agree that what is happening today, before our very eyes, is what was predicted in earlier times by the prophets and sages. Thus a man could, as it were, take the Bible in his right hand and the evening paper in his left and he would be reading the same thing in both. We increasingly hear of attempts to calculate the onset of the final redemption, with fragmentary citations of biblical verses, whether their literal meaning or allusions, and even numerology. According to believers in this approach, everything that was foreseen corresponds not only to the general historical picture but also to its details, such as the 1956 Sinai campaign, the subsequent withdrawal from Sinai, the 1967 Six Day War, etc. The prophetic approach looks out, so to speak, from a mountaintop into the distance. That elevated vista includes, of course, both the Holocaust and the reborn state. It foresaw and foretold those events and it now claims to know how to define and interpret everything that happens. It sees the hand of God in history and the state of Israel in the light of the vision of redemption and the coming of the messiah.

As opposed to the "positive prophetic approach," there is a "negative prophetic approach" which also claims to occupy a prophetic peak from which it discerns a meaning in every event. It too sees the hand of God in history, but arrives at a completely different assessment. In this view, what we are seeing now is no miracle but rather a trial which God is placing before us, the establishment of the state belittles the universal vision of the prophets, the building up of the land is a flight from the ideal situation of existence in the diaspora, returning to the family of nations is a betrayal of our particular mission, and our victories on the battlefield are an insult to our sublime self-image.

The "midrashic approach," like the "prophetic approach," contemplates events in the light of what has been said and written in previous ages—but it is different in that it does not assume to interpret authoritatively and categorically the meaning of specific events. Rather, it seeks to associate developments in our time with past visions and to interpret the present on the basis of those visions. Not everything is explicit, obvious, or self-evident in the history of recent generations. On the contrary, more things are obscure than certain, more is in pieces than in place. The most recent period is entirely problematic, one paradox on top of another, but that is the path of Midrash: to live with contradictions. Two verses refute each other, and a third comes along to resolve the differences between the two. Miracles? In itself Jewish existence is miraculous. As every Jew experiences in his own life, the meta-historical touches upon the historical. Individual as well as collective Jewish consciousness is permeated, as Emil Fackenheim has taught us, with that root experience, and the state of Israel reverberates with the voice bursting forth from Auschwitz, proclaiming the six hundred and fourteenth commandment, the one that follows the 613 positive and negative precepts, crying out: LIVE! The Israeli pioneers who make the desert bloom in our times respond to an echo of the poetic prophecies, describing luxuriant greenery, in the books of Isaiah, Jeremiah, and Zephaniah, with images of the joyful desert and the blooming valley, the mountains that drip with nectar and the hills that melt.

So much of what the prophets and sages envisioned and foretold is being realized before our very eyes. But on the other hand, a great deal of what they foresaw is *not* happening, at least not yet. How are we to understand that? We are compelled to live with constant doubt. A brief examination of the list of the signs of universal and particular redemption, as they have been given to us by our prophets and sages, shows that only a small number of them have occurred, and most of those only in part. The developments which will unfold when the messiah comes include, for example:

1. peace among the nations
2. ecological peace, that is, harmony in nature

3. universal education and knowledge
4. economic equality and plenty
5. universal justice
6. religious freedom
7. Zion and Jerusalem as a center of Torah, from which will radiate knowledge of the word of God

Those are the seven universal signs, to which these particularistic ones, applicable to the Jewish condition, should be added:

8. exodus from servitude to freedom
9. ingathering of the exiles
10. rebuilding of Jerusalem and the Temple
11. flourishing of the land of Israel
12. restoration of the Davidic monarchy

Those who believe in the "midrashic approach" examine this list and wonder at the gap between what has been achieved and what we desire and hope for, concluding that we have gone but a little way. Nonetheless, the accomplishments already realized must be taken into account and interpreted. The midrashic view naturally does not yield clear-cut, unequivocal answers. The Torah and reality have seventy "faces," some positive and others negative.

The last of our typological categories is the "halakhic approach." We do not refer to those rabbinic scholars who decide upon matters of Halakha (Jewish religious law), but rather to a general approach that is essentially halakhic in nature. Instead of adopting a broad metahistorical or metaphysical point of view, it poses a practical halakhic question: Now that the state exists as a given which impinges on the Jewish world in radical ways, what must I, as a faithful Jew, do?

Of course, it is impossible to answer that practical question without seeking some definition and comprehension of the given, existing situation. For that purpose, this approach does not need to unfurl the vast canvas of prophecy embracing the whole nation and the world. A realistic description of the new existing situation is generally sufficient. And that description entails a great many practical halakhic consequences. For example, on Israel Independence Day, should one adopt the liturgical expressions mandated for festivals and recite the *Hallel* (the song of thanksgiving comprising verses from the psalms) or the *Shehechiyanu* blessing for having reached the present moment? For a religious Jew, that is not a neutral, purely theoretical question. The answer to it determines whether one is obligated to recite them (and, therefore, may not refrain from doing so), or, antithetically whether one is *not* obligated to do so, in which case one would be reciting a blessing in vain.

There are many similar issues, not all of them in the ritual area. For example, what is the halakhic definition of the wars waged by the state? If they do not belong to the category of *milhemet mitzva* (a war which one is commanded to fight), one might be committing murder or willful destruction if one takes part in them. Or: Can the Israeli economy today accommodate national observance of the sabbatical or jubilee years, or even the grounding of El Al airlines on the sabbath? The essential issue here is whether halakhic norms that governed personal or communal life under diaspora conditions can be applied without adaptation or reinterpretation in present-day Israel.

Not all the sages of the Talmud adopted the "halakhic approach." Rabbi Akiba, doubtless one of the greatest sages of the oral tradition, was closer to the prophetic approach when he proclaimed that Bar Kokhba was the messianic king, basing his belief in a visionary poetical verse: "A star (*kokhav*) shall come forth out of Jacob" (Num 24:17). Nevertheless, in general, the rabbis speak of redemption and the messiah from the point of view of halakhic reality. Thus Rabbi Yohanan, who lived in Tiberias in the early third century, says: "When you see a generation which is ever dwindling—await Him . . . when you see a generation overwhelmed by tribulations as by a river—await Him."[8] Other sages of those generations spoke in similar fashion. Ze'iri said in the name of Rabbi Hanina: "The Son of David shall not come until there will be no more coarse-natured people in Israel."[9] Rabbi Simlai said in the name of Rabbi Elazar, the son of Rabbi Simeon: "The Son of David shall not come until all the judges and officers are gone from Israel."[10] In these quotations the rabbis do not amuse themselves with enchanting illusions, but they instead express hopes and, at the same time, incisive social criticism referring to their particular place and time. Messianic hopes flourished in a cruel and tragic setting, leading the sages of the Talmud to express themselves with sharp irony, which is especially conspicuous in contrast to the eschatological statements of their predecessors, the prophets. One famous example is the following:

In the footsteps of the Messiah, insolence shall increase, honor shall be perverted, the vine shall give of its fruit but wine will be expensive, the government shall become heretical, and no one shall reprimand it; acad-

emies shall become houses of ill-repute, the Galilee shall be destroyed
and Gablan desolated, and dwellers from the borders will go from city
to city, and none shall take pity on them; the wisdom of the learned
shall degenerate, those who fear sin shall be despised and truth shall be
lacking; youths shall shame their elders, the old shall rise in deference to
the young; a son shall disgrace his father, a daughter rebel against her
mother, the wife against her mother-in-law; a man's enemies shall be
from his own household, and the face of the generation shall be like a
dog's face; the son shall not feel ashamed before his father, so upon
whom shall we depend?—upon our Father in heaven.[11]

In examining the matter of redemption they recognized that it entails
various considerations and that one possibility of the messiah's coming is
unlike another. Rabbi Joshua ben Levi juxtaposed two verses from the
Bible. In one, it is written, "One like a son of man came with the clouds of
heaven" (Dan 7:13), and the second verse states, "Poor and riding upon a
donkey" (Zec 9:9). Apparently there is a contradiction between these two
verses which speak of the coming of the messiah. In one he arrives in great
honor and glory, with the clouds of heaven which move quickly, and in
the second he is poor and rides upon a donkey, making slow progress, and
hardly respectable. Rabbi Joshua ben Levi's reconciling answer is: If the
Jews have great merit, then he will come like the clouds of heaven; and if
they do not have great merit, riding on a donkey. The messiah shall certainly come, but what a huge difference there is between "meriting" him
and not doing so! The actual circumstances will determine the way in
which he arrives.

Nevertheless, actual circumstances did not dim the sages' excitement
at the great prospects inherent within real history nor extinguish their
hopes for total redemption. That very Rabbi Yohanan, who awaited the
coming of the messiah in a flow of troubles as mighty as a river, also
becomes very excited and says: "The ingathering of the exiles will be as
great a day as that in which the heavens and the earth were created,"[12] and
his colleague Rabbi Abba, in the midst of the same troubled time, points
out that the end is at hand, saying: "There can be no clearer sign of
redemption than this, namely, what is said in Ezekiel 36:8, 'But you, O
mountains of Israel, you shall shoot forth your branches and yield your
fruit to my people Israel, for they will soon be coming.' "[13] The quotation
from Ezekiel continues: "For, behold, I am for you, and I will turn to you,
and you shall be tilled and sown. I will plant many men upon you, the
whole house of Israel. The cities shall again be inhabited and the waste
places rebuilt." In the very fact of rebuilding the ruins, working the land,

and making the trees blossom in the land of Israel, the redemption is at hand.

The halakhic approach does not seek to answer the question "What is the redemption?" but rather "What must I do?" It is concerned with the essence of the matter only to the extent that it influences action, and therefore it is important to this outlook, no less than to the prophetic approach, to find a halakhic-religious response and orientation applicable to that historical period in which an independent Jewish commonwealth exists. Is the agricultural and economic flourishing of the land of Israel actually a sign that the messianic end is at hand? If so, what does that situation obligate me to do? The challenge confronting those who take the halakhic approach is a difficult one, in that it presupposes a stance which is basic to the application of Halakha, namely, the axiom that "it is not in heaven,"[14] i.e. that the Torah has already been given at Mount Sinai, and no divine intervention in this world, including miracles, signs, and wonders, will supersede it. All the answers and all the solutions must be found here and now. There is no room for miracles in the Halakha, as it is explicitly stated in the Talmud: "One must not rely on miracles."[15] The problem faced by those who adopt the halakhic approach in relation to the new historical given known as the state of Israel is not in the area of miracles, but rather in a new, factual reality the likes of which have not existed before. What is the existential meaning of that reality? To what does it obligate us, in actual practice?

The traditional view of Jewish history conceives of three possible states of national existence:

A. The Temple period including both first and second Temples. It is a direct continuation of the exodus from Egypt. During this period the Temple was intact—it was a period of fulfillment, with both high points and low ones from the time of Joshua until that of the final destruction in 70 C.E.

B. The period of exile from the destruction of the second Temple until our times. That period was characterized by crises and disintegration, the loss of independence, the shutting off of the sources of prophecy, and prayer and hope for redemption and for a messiah—"Though he tarry I daily wait for him."

C. The messianic period, the return to a "mended" world, the reconstruction of the Temple as it was, the return of the divine presence to Zion and of our judges as in the early days and our counselors as at the beginning: "Renew our days as of old," our prayer implores—that is, a full-scale return to the glory and splendor of period A.

Yet a problem arises: Is there room within that framework for yet another period, a fourth one, which is not yet messianic (for the halakhic approach is denied the right and the authority inherent in the prophetic approach of terming this period a messianic age), but no longer one of exile, for we are in our own land, and the hand of Israel is sovereign, a period in which the Temple is not being rebuilt but during which it is also difficult to weep for the destruction of Jerusalem the violated and destroyed, "humiliated and cast down to sheol" (cf Jer 14:17)?

The question with regard to this interim period is a new one, but not entirely new. Some authorities hold that, with regard to this issue, the sages of the Talmud were divided during the time of Bar Kokhba, as were some of the greatest rabbis during following generations, as to whether the very fact of Jewish rule in the land of Israel or of victories in wars of reconquest against an aggressor has the power of giving religious sanction to events.[16] That is the essence of the dispute between Rabbi Akiba, who called Bar Kokhba the messianic king, and Rabbi Yohanan Ben Torta, who protested and called out: "Akiba, weeds will sprout from your cheeks and still the Son of David shall not come!"[17] Maimonides agrees, apparently, with Rabbi Akiba regarding the messianic criteria applied to Bar Kokhba, with one halakhic reservation—for ultimately the test of a messiah is that of reality, "If he acted and succeeded . . . then he is definitely the messiah," and in the case of Bar Kokhba, "Since he was killed, they knew that he was not."[18] Rashi expresses reservations in his commentary on the Talmud about attributing messianic status to Bar Kokhba and the period of his rule, "For we have seen several Jewish kingdoms after the destruction, but nevertheless the messiah did not come."[19]

The sages of the Talmud and the Halakha did not reach a final decision. They were cautious about soaring off on the wings of apocalyptic imagination, although they did transmit to us their realistic expectations and hopes with regard to the question. They instructed us that the redemption is not a question of all or nothing, but little by little. The inspiration for that conception arose from personal observation of the landscape around them. They did not come to a vision of redemption on the basis of distant speculations about the faraway heavens—but during their travels within the actual land of Israel they were filled with a strong feeling that the redemption of Israel was imminent. "Rabbi Hiyya the Great and

Rabbi Simeon ben Halafta were walking in the Arbel Valley, and they saw the morning star give forth its light. Rabbi Hiyya the Great said to Rabbi Simeon: Rabbi, thus is the Redemption of Israel—first little by little, but as it continues advancing, it becomes greater and greater."[20]

In Jewish prayers, as formulated in the liturgy, there is no plea for a sudden, colossal outburst of redemption, but for a certain order in the process of redemption, and the rabbis sought to anchor that order in one of the formal structures basic to Jewish thought, the *Amidah* prayer. Also known as the Eighteen Benedictions, it is the backbone of daily prayer whose essence is the act of "ordering" which preceded its official standardization. It is written: "Simeon Hapakuli arranged the Eighteen Benedictions before Rabban Gamliel according to the order in Yavneh."[21] The Talmud explained the order of the prayers in the Eighteen Benedictions in the following fashion: "As it is taught: one hundred and twenty elders, including several prophets, arranged the Eighteen Benedictions in their *order*."[22] Their hopes and their aspirations for redemption were rooted in the soil of reality, and they taught that it would come gradually, step by step. One stage will flow from another in a sort of cause-and-effect sequence, and this is the order of events which emerges from the Eighteen Benedictions:

> Repentance follows understanding, forgiveness follows repentance, and then—redemption. And why did they pray for the ingathering of the exiles after the prayer for a fruitful year? As it is written in Ezekiel 36:8, "But you, O mountains of Israel, you shall shoot forth your branches and yield your fruit to my people Israel, for they will soon be coming." And once the exiles are gathered in (Ez 36:24.28), the evil-doers will be brought to justice, as it is written in Isaiah 1:25–26, "I will turn my hand against you, and purge away the dross as with lye . . . and I will restore your judges as at the first." And once the wicked have been brought to judgment, there will be no more sinners, and once there are no more sinners, the righteous will flourish, and where shall the righteous flourish? In Jerusalem, as it is said in Psalm 122:6: "Pray for the peace of Jerusalem; they who love you shall prosper." And once Jerusalem is rebuilt, David shall come, as it is written in Hosea 3:5, "After the children of Israel have returned, they shall ask for the Lord and for David, their king." And after David appears, prayer will be restored to its rightful place, as it is written in Isaiah 56:7, "And I will bring them to my holy mountain and make them joyful in my house of prayer." And with the return of prayer will come the return of the temple service, as it is written, "Their offerings and sacrifices will be accepted upon my altar" (ibid). After the restoration of the temple service will come the

thanksgiving offering. And why does the prayer for peace follow the priestly blessing? As it is written (Num 6:27): "And they shall put my name upon the children of Israel and I shall bless them." What is God's blessing? Peace, as it is written Psalm 29:11, "The Lord will bless his people with peace."[23]

That order of redemption does not indicate that the rabbis gave up hope for a total, eschatological redemption; however, it does take place in the real world, the concrete world which is the realm of the Halakha. The Halakha demands that one walk with an assured and measured step in the world, without the pathos and fire of the prophets, in painful knowledge that we possess neither the Temple nor the altar, neither the fragrant offerings nor the fire offerings, but we can progress toward them—in fact we are obligated to do so. Thus the commandment to settle the land of Israel applies to all times—even today—with all its quotidian ramifications, so that one should feel "the Temple shall soon be restored" by means of a series of concrete acts which express a quiet love for the land of Israel, her very trees and stones.

Many halakhic enactments are intertwined with the comprehensive theme of progress toward complete redemption, but from the time of the sages until the present the matter was not spoken about explicitly. From time to time, we find outbursts of messianism which end in bitter disillusionment, and we also find the beginnings of political reestablishment on the land—but they never got beyond mere beginnings. In our days, there are those who claim that Zionism, which brought about the establishment of the state of Israel, is a national, political, and secular movement, the product of the historical conditions of the nineteenth century, whereas others claim that it is essentially an outgrowth of the deep religious bond between Judaism and the land of Israel, a bond to which all the classical halakhic sources bear witness, as do the Aggadah and the liturgy. According to that view, Pinsker and Herzl were not the first Zionists, but rather they stood in the tradition of the patriarch Abraham, who obeyed God's command and set forth toward the land (Gen 12:1), and Moses our teacher, who begged to cross over and see the good land (Dt 3:23), and Rabbi Simeon Bar Yohai who viewed the land of Israel as a gift of God together with the Torah and the world to come,[24] and Rabbi Abba who kissed the stones of Acco, and Rabbi Hiyya Bar Gamda who rolled about in its dust,[25] and Rabbi Judah Halevi (eleventh–twelfth centuries), greatest of the poets of Zion, and Rabbi Haim Ben Atar who went up to the land of Israel in the eighteenth century with a messianic impulse, and all of the other wise, righteous, and pious Jews who poured out their longings for the land of Israel and went up to it from all over the world to reclaim the earth and rebuild its ruins. Anyone who examines the roots of the Zionist movement and the patterns of its growth will find two interrelated factors, both the secular-national and the religious-messianic, that mutually reinforced one another. Religious Zionism is not the exclusive property of those people who call themselves "religious," but it is a basic foundation stone in the lives of many Jews who carry out their Zionism in practice—both those who are called "religious" and those who are termed "non-religious." The return to the land of the Bible was, to a great extent, a return to the Bible itself, both to its language and its content. Identification with Zionism was necessarily an identification—or at least an existential confrontation—with Judaism, its heritage, its fate, and its aspirations.

Any attempt to give a religious definition of the state of Israel, which is of course the product of the Zionist movement, must speculate about the religious essence of Zionism. It must free itself of the commonplace division of Zionism into religious and secular streams and not judge the religiosity of the state of Israel according to the extent of Orthodox representation in the political framework of the state. A person can be religious and a Zionist, but that does not necessarily make him a religious Zionist in the truest sense, i.e. his identification with the state of Israel is an integral part of his spirituality and his religious convictions encompass the ideals and practical demands of Zionism. Similarly, in his private life and in the voting booth a person may reject the commandments defined by Halakha, and especially their application to the political life of the state, yet he can nevertheless act out of a deeply held religious Zionism.

The forefathers of the Zionist movement in the nineteenth century, Rabbis Alkalai, Kalischer, Mohilever, and Eliasberg, do not belong exclusively in the National Religious Party, just as Moses Hess, Heinrich Graetz, and Peretz Smolenskin do not belong merely to the secular branch of the Zionist movement. The Zionist movement, in all its parts, was nourished by deep, historical religious roots, and it was permeated by the vision of the Hebrew prophets. From its start, this movement represented a modern reflection of the classical triangle comprising God, the Jewish people, and Zion, a triangle that rests upon an unbroken Jewish faith. Even those who distanced themselves from the religion or who did not know the verses were nourished directly or indirectly by such biblical quotations as: "A land which the Lord, your God, cares for always; the eyes of the Lord, your God, are upon it from the beginning of the year till the end of it" (Dt 11:12), or by the prophets, where the land of Israel is called "the land of their possession . . . by the word of God" (Jos 22:9).

All their requests and expectations for the betterment of the world and of mankind were directed toward it, as these Zionist pioneers derived their inspiration from scripture, which overflows with yearning for the scenery of Zion and Israel, as in the Song of Songs, and from the intense longing for Jerusalem which permeates the Psalms. "Ask for the peace of Jerusalem, may those who love you prosper" (Ps 122:6). In Jewish consciousness the land of Israel was always the land of destiny and promise, the cradle of holiness, the land from which, because of our sins, we were exiled and distanced, and to which we yearn and aspire to return at all times.

The dispute over the religious or secular nature of Zionism is not a new one; it can be found in Zionist and anti-Zionist thought almost from the very beginnings of the movement. The innovation inherent in the establishment of the state of Israel lies in the fact that history has caught up to thought and gone beyond it. The fifth of Iyyar, 5708, is the watershed. From then on, the theoretical debate over whether the establishment of an independent state is part of the "ultimate aim" of Zionism is over. The Jewish state is a fact. The problem reverts to its proper focus: Is that state, as it is, a "chance" occurrence or even an historical "accident," with no consequences at all for Jewish thought, or should it have a significant impact on that thought? And if so, just what is its significance?

Almost all of the answers proposed to those questions adhere to the classical model of redemption and the messianic era. We have seen the various possibilities that are inherent in that attempt, possibilities that are conditioned by the point of departure and upon the particular approach, whether it be prophetic, midrashic, or halakhic, positive or negative. Every answer which has been proposed in light of the confrontation of the state of Israel with the messianic dream is either predictable or else leads us up a blind alley. However, it seems to me that it is possible to seek religious significance within the structure of Jewish self-understanding without being bound to the classical model of redemption—and that is what we shall seek to do in what follows, by juxtaposing the state as an historical reality with some of the basic values of Jewish faith and religion, without resorting to the theological categories of messiah, miracle, redemption, etc.

It has been aptly said that to be a Jew is to live with a calendar in one's hand. The sabbaths and festivals in that calendar not only unite us with the past; they also represent a focus and a challenge for the present and future. The sabbath is a memorial of the act of creation, but it is also a challenge for man as the creature of God, for on the sabbath a man leaves the created world of which he is a part and participates in the creation of the world, his own world, whose challenge is not to be identified with what he does, but with what he is. Existence precedes action. Passover does not merely celebrate the exodus from Egypt in the distant past, but it confronts us with freedom as a challenge in our daily lives; and that is also the case with Shavuot, the holiday which commemorates the giving of the Torah in the past, at Mount Sinai, and also presents the challenge of it today. The other Jewish holidays are of a similar nature. Instead of studying a catechism that defines the principles of his faith, the Jew is commanded to live an ongoing religious life all year long, a life whose focal points are marked on the calendar.

An additional holiday has been added to that calendar in recent years, Israel Independence Day, the fifth of Iyyar (or, when it falls on a sabbath, the preceding Thursday). Since the first Independence Day, there has been constant discussion among the Torah sages in the Jewish world as to how to mark the day liturgically, just as the other festivals in the Jewish calendar have their liturgical characteristics. All those who participate in that discussion agree that the holiday cannot possess national-historical meaning alone, commemorating what happened on one specific date, the fifth of Iyyar, 5708. Everyone senses that if Israel Independence Day actually does become an integral part of the Jewish calendar—and all the indications are that it is on the way to being integrated as such—then it must represent some basic Jewish value which is connected to that day, a value which, in the course of time, will become an educational and spiritual challenge that one reexperiences anew on that date every year.

We shall see that the values and challenges connected with the appearance of an independent Jewish state at this point in Jewish and world history are manifold. However, it is not necessarily in the complex confrontation with the variegated messianic dimension that we find the answer.

Matters would be simple if everyone could view Independence Day as a holiday of redemption without "slipping into" prophetical thinking. The expression which appears in the official prayer for the welfare of the state, describing it as "the beginning of the sprouting of our redemption," is intentionally modest, cautious, and does not obligate one to a particular view.

Perhaps we can clarify the matter by examining the concept which is antithetical to that of redemption, i.e. exile, *galut.* Did the establishment of the state bring about a change in that concept?

It is well known that secular, political Zionism grew principally out of a negative diagnosis of Jewish life in the diaspora. It was the rejection of the diaspora as a desirable and permanent condition, worthy of continuing indefinitely or until the messiah comes to a passive Jewish people, which led to the Zionist solution to the problem of exile by emigration to the land of Israel. Just as redemption was an ancient ingredient of the Jewish mythos, so was exile. And just as the exodus from Egypt was an archetype of redemption, so was servitude in Egypt the archetype of exile. In the Jewish mythical conception, the first redemption, which culminated in the conquest and the settlement of the land of Israel, is a conditional redemption. If the conditions are not fulfilled, if the Torah and its commandments are not observed, then exile will follow. The principal characteristic of exile is, therefore, that it is a punishment, one that still contains a promise of ultimate redemption, i.e. the deliverance from exile. That dialectical situation of life in exile accompanied by fervent adherence to the promise, the hope, and the prayer for redemption characterizes most of the long history of the Jewish people. Exile is both a strong feeling and the objective lack of a homeland and of citizenship, or a condition of second-class citizenship as an alien in someone else's society. In short, it is an unnatural existence, lacking inner security and, at times, also physical safety. When, during the long years of exile, the idea of leaving one's place of residence sometimes arose, or it became necessary to do so, it generally led to migration to another place of exile. The wandering Jew, moving from one land of exile to another, symbolized a curse in the eyes of Christians, while it enriched and varied Jewish history with frequent encounters with different cultures.

The state of Israel, which enacted the Law of Return at its outset, making it possible for every Jew to "return home," thereby declared that it was the antithesis of exile. The emphasis placed by the state during the first years of its existence was upon the "ingathering of the exiles," as it arranged for the immigration of hundreds of thousands of Jews. Some of them made *aliya* (return to Israel) because of their sufferings in exile or because of the ancient messianic vision, and for them modern Zionism was entirely unknown. This massive ingathering fortified the claim that the very existence of the old-new state put an end to the exile, at least according to the classical definition, that is, a coercive and imperfect existential situation lacking Jewish fulfillment—if not for every individual Jew, certainly with regard to the people as a whole. Now the Jew is no longer required to live in exile. If he leaves one place of exile, he need not go to another one. The land of Israel and a nation of Jews await him.

When Jews leave their place of exile in order to return to the land of Israel, that is a religious act, since the exile of the Jews is conceived of as a religious event, not only a national and political one: punishment for their sins. The possibility which is now envisaged of terminating the period of exile in the life of the Jewish people is both a theoretical possibility and also a practical and feasible one, not only because there is a state of Israel which has opened its gates to Jews and thus says to them, "Exile as punishment has ceased, and henceforth there is only exile as a choice," but also because the exile is gradually withering away as a result of accelerated assimilation. The radical possibility to make *aliya* to a Jewish state has raised the formerly theoretical discussion to the level of a practical, immediate, religious issue, which no Jew who is faithful to his tradition may avoid.

We are not discussing the positive commandment to settle the land of Israel, but rather the astonishing phenomenon of willfully remaining in exile when the possibility exists for leaving it. What justification is there today for a Jew to say, like the slave whose ear is pierced, "I love my master . . . and I shall not go forth free" (Ex 21:5)? While exile is a punishment, it is certainly not a commandment!

The Talmud states that "God did a charitable deed for the Jewish people by scattering them among the nations" because the Jew's life-destiny is to live among the Gentiles in order to disseminate the true religion among all the nations. And a corollary: "God did not exile the Jews among the nations except in order that converts join their numbers."[26] But what religious duty or benefit can there be today, after the Holocaust and in the midst of the hemorrhage of assimilation by continued Jewish life in exile? We are not speaking of indolence or objective conditions that may make a given Jew's *aliya* difficult, but of a general religious justification for communal Jewish life in exile today.

"And because of our sins we were exiled from our land," say the Jews every sabbath and holiday. Perhaps to remain in exile when there is the possibility of leaving actually turns the original punishment for sin into a new sin. At the beginning of the modern era, many years before Zionist thought made us aware of the abnormality of life in exile, one of the greatest Jewish thinkers, the Maharal of Prague (d. 1609) wrote:

> There is no doubt that exile is a change and a departure from order. For
> the Lord, blessed be He, placed every nation in the place worthy of it

and also placed the Jews in the place worthy of them, which is the Land of Israel. For that place which is worthy of them according to the order of reality is that they be in the Land of Israel under their own jurisdiction. . . . And similarly their dispersion is not a natural thing. . . . Therefore the dispersion of the Jews among the nations is something unnatural, since they are one nation and ought to stand together and be one. . . . Moreover . . . according to the order of reality one nation ought not to be subjected to another in servitude with a heavy yoke upon it, for the Lord, blessed be He, created every nation for its own sake. . . . And if it were to remain the case forever, that is, the exile and the hand of other nations ruling over Israel, that would be something opposed to the order of reality. Thus from exile we can perceive redemption.[27]

In the same vein, more than a century after the Maharal, another great scholar condemned the condition of exile in modern times from a religious point of view. Rabbi Jacob Emden (1697–1776) cried out:

Therefore pay heed to me, my brothers and comrades who live in a land which is not ours and on polluted soil. . . . Hasten, draw nigh, and act. Do not think of settling outside of the Land of Israel, heaven forfend . . . to carry out the prophecy that the land of your enemies shall devour you. . . . That was the sin of your forefathers, a cause for generations of mourning, for they rejected the beloved land. . . . It seems to us, while we live in peace outside of the Land of Israel, that we have already found another Israel and another Jerusalem in their place. Therefore all those evils came upon us when the Jews dwelled in Spain and in other lands in tranquillity and with great honor. . . . And once again they were driven out, so that there is no remnant of the Jews in that land.[28]

Those words were addressed to the Jews of eighteenth century Germany, and today they sound like a prophetic warning to all those who reject the beloved land and choose exile, instead of going up to the land of Israel. An ever stiffer argument than that can be heard from a great rabbi of our generation, Rabbi Haim David Halevi, the chief rabbi of Tel Aviv-Jaffa, who holds, "The end of exile is destruction." He claims that it is written explicitly: "And you shall be lost among the Gentiles and the land of your enemies shall devour you" (Lev 26:38). In his opinion, to leave the exile today is a matter of saving lives, which is, without doubt, a religious duty. We must flee from exile, Rabbi Halevi claims, if we wish to be saved from that which befell the Jews who were killed during the Holocaust.

Because they did not hasten to put an end to exile, exile put an end to them, in accordance with the dreadful prophecy of Ezekiel 20:38: "From the land where they sojourn shall I remove them, and to the soil of Israel they shall not come."

In the story of the exodus from Egypt it is told that all those children of Israel who did not wish to go forth died during the three days of darkness. Rabbi Halevi asks: "Why so drastic a measure? Why not take out those who wished to go, and whoever wished to remain could live honorably in the Egyptian diaspora? The conclusion is clear, that there could have been no full redemption unless all the Jews went up from Egypt." Also during the time of the second Temple there was no complete redemption because only a small number of people went up from Babylon, and thus the Talmud cries out: "If you had made a bastion of yourselves and gone up, all of you, during the days of Ezra, you would have been as sovereign as untarnished silver."[29]

So Rabbi Halevi, from examining the destruction of the Temple, the rebellion of Bar Kokhba, and the suppression of that rebellion, arrives at this conclusion: "It was not the destruction of the temple that caused the exile, but rather the opposite is the case: the exile caused the destruction of the Temple, with all its consequences."[30]

Leaving exile in order to return to the land of Israel is a central motif in all of Jewish liturgy. Throughout all generations, the land was the focus of the nation's yearnings, impelling many pious people to attempt to put them into effect, by going to the land of Israel and paying homage to its sacred soil. This was immigration on the part of individuals in a continuous trickle to Zion. We do not know of any ideological reasons that would have prevented a mass return to the land. Rather, the objective conditions that then held in the world and in the land of Israel would seem to explain the low number of returnees.

Even those authors of the *Tosafot* (Talmudic commentaries) who held that the commandment to settle the land of Israel does not hold in our times said so only because of the dangers or difficulties inherent in carrying out that commandment under the conditions then prevailing. Today, now that the gates of Israel are open, and the danger of remaining in many lands is greater than that of journeying to Israel, one must be amazed that there are Jews who do not leave the exile, for they thus indicate that their own prayers and those of their ancestors were recited insincerely. They cry out, "Bring us back," and "Make us return!" Twice a year, on Passover and Yom Kippur, they declare in unison, "Next year in Jerusalem"—but they continue to settle more and more firmly in Gentile lands.

The paradox of Jewish life in exile today has been intentionally repressed, and it would almost seem as if world Jewry swore to keep silent about it. Whenever a challenge is raised, efforts are made to refute it with clever semantic and historical arguments about the differences between "diaspora" and "exile," and about historical precedents for existence of an independent Jewish state with the parallel existence of a large diaspora. If such arguments have a place in Jewish historiography (and an investigation is called for concerning the physical and social costs of the various "diasporas"), they certainly have none in Jewish religious thought, which, so far as is known to us, does not acknowledge the status of exile-which-is-not exile. The problematic issue of defining the present status of Jewry outside the land of Israel is less complex than the religious definition of the Jewish state.

An exception to that generalization is presented by the religious anti-Zionists, who are consistent in their view of present day Jewish existence as exile (everywhere—even in Jerusalem), with all that that entails, and who separate themselves from the nation in whose midst they dwell, closing themselves off within their self-made ghetto. They justify their anti-Zionism by claiming that it is forbidden to cooperate with secular, non-observant Jews such as the Zionist leaders and pioneers who carried out the practical work of nation-building. Some of the ultra-Orthodox Jews have found additional justification in a rabbinical statement, in which there is an interpretation of the verse in the Song of Songs (2:7): "I charge you, O daughters of Jerusalem, by the gazelles and by the hinds of the field, that you not stir up, nor awake my love till it pleases." Since expressions for swearing an oath appear three times in that context, Rabbi Yose beRabi Hanina gave the following interpretation: " 'What are the three oaths? One, that they not go up to Israel like a wall (i.e. together, by force); the second, that the Holy One, Blessed be He, made Israel swear not to rebel against the nations of the world; and the third, that the Holy One, Blessed be He, made the nations of the world swear that they would not subjugate Israel excessively.' ... Rabbi Elazar said: 'The Holy One, Blessed be He, said to Israel, if you abide by your oath, it will be well with you, but if not, I will permit your flesh to be eaten like that of the gazelles and the hinds of the field.' "[31] On that basis the Neturei Karta zealots and Satmar Hasidim have ruled, "One must fight against a Jewish state in the land of Israel, even if its leaders are observers of the Torah and its commandments, for the very idea of a state is utter blasphemy, since it was established on the basis of violating an oath."[32]

Around that aggadic quotation (for it does not appear in a halakhic context), which is used to support the argument against immigrating to the land of Israel at the present time, an extensive literature has been created concerning whether the establishment of the state—and even before that, the Zionist enterprise—entailed "going up like a wall" and/or "rebellion against the nations." Those who argue against the use of that rabbinical quotation to deny the legitimacy of the state from a religious point of view aver that the establishment of the state was confirmed by a vote of two-thirds of the members of the United Nations on November 29, 1947, and therefore it cannot be a rebellion against the nations. Moreover, we do not have merely a single oath here, but a triple one which appears as a single unit; and it was violated first of all by the nations of the world, who did subjugate the Jews excessively during the period of the Holocaust. Since the oath was violated from their side, it is entirely void and no longer obligates us.

Still, this entire polemical dispute among the Orthodox fails to address the basic question that can not be dismissed through clever semantics, and that keeps challenging those Jews who observe the Torah and its commandments. This key issue of Jewish integrity—meshing prayer with deed—is put by Rabbi Judah Halevi into the mouth of the Khazar king. The king asks it of the "rabbi" after the latter has extolled the act of making *aliya* to the land of Israel:

> If this be so, you fall short of the duty laid down in your Torah, by not endeavoring to reach that place, and making it your abode in life and death, although you say, "Have mercy on Zion, for it is the house of our life," and believe that the Shekhinah will return there. Is it not the "Gate of Heaven"? All the nations agree on this point. . . . All men direct their prayers to that place and make pilgrimages to it. Therefore your bowing down in its direction is mere hypocrisy or a religious act that is not fully intended.[33]

The "rabbi's" answer is one that today very few people have the courage to make sincerely:

> Truly you have found something shameful in me, O King of the Kuzaris! For that is the sin which thwarted the divine promise of the second temple: "Be joyful and be glad, O daughter of heaven, for I am

coming to dwell within you, saith the Lord" (Zec 2:10). The divine presence was ready to return to them as in the early days, if all of them had consented and returned to the land of Israel with bold souls. But only some of them responded, while most of them, including the most eminent among them, remained in Babylon, preferring exile and servitude rather than be separated from their houses and their businesses.[34]

Rabbi Judah Halevi wrote those words around the year 1140, long before the reemergence of the state of Israel. Even then he made the claim that to the degree that the Jews roused themselves and acted to bring about the redemption, redemption would come, and with it the divine presence. Judah Halevi, the "rabbi," does not reject that accusation of the Khazar king. He does not seek to justify the continuation of exile. He agrees completely with the king's description of the Jews as "a body without head or heart." "Yes, it is as you say, even more—we are not even a body, only limbs, like the 'dry bones' of Ezekiel's vision."[35] But despite that negative and pessimistic appraisal of the exilic situation, Halevi, the "rabbi," does not lose all hope for the Jewish future. To this very day, his words can be a source of encouragement for Zionism as a program of concrete action even in its darkest moments, periods of decline and fall, which it is not spared from time to time.

After all their discussions, the "rabbi" makes up his mind, as it is told in the Afterword, "to leave the land of the Khazars and to journey to Jerusalem, may it be rebuilt and restored." The departure of the "rabbi" was difficult for the Khazar king, who said, "What can you find in the land of Israel today, for the divine presence is absent from it? Whereas closeness to God is possible anywhere by means of a pure heart and a strong desire for it. So why do you risk the dangers of the deserts and the seas and the hatred of various nations?"

Those arguments and many others do not prevent the "rabbi" from setting forth on his way. If it is possible to identify the "rabbi" in the *Kuzari* with the author, Judah Halevi, then we ought to add the biographical conclusion which folk literature has spun about his death. When he arrived, after a very long journey, at the gates of Jerusalem, Rabbi Judah Halevi began to recite one of his poems, filled with yearning: "Zion, dost thou not ask after the well-being of thy prisoners?" At that very moment, an Arab horseman galloped by on his charger and trampled Judah Halevi to death.

Thus the poet reached the gates of the holy city for which he yearned, but he did not enter it.

NOTES

1. The twelve oracular stones on the breastplate of the high priest (cf. Ex 28:30; Lev 8:8).
2. TB *Berakhot* 34b.
3. Ibid.; cf. also *Sanhedrin* 91b and 99a.
4. *Hilkhot Melakhim* 12,2.
5. Ibid. 11,3.
6. Ibid. 11,4.
7. TB *Berakhot* 4a.
8. TB *Sanhedrin* 98a.
9. Ibid.
10. Ibid.
11. TB *Sotah* 49b.
12. TB *Pesahim* 88a.
13. TB *Sanhedrin* 98a.
14. TB *Baba Metziah* 59b, citing Dt 30:12.
15. TB *Pesahim* 64b.
16. Rabbi Shlomo Goren, "The State of Israel as a Stage in the Vision of the Prophets of Israel," in *Mahanayim* 45, for Israel Independence Day 5720 (1950).
17. TJ *Ta'anit* 4,5 and *Eikhah Rabbati* 3.
18. *Hilkhot Melakhim* 11,4.
19. TB *Sanhedrin* 97b.
20. TJ *Berakhot* 1,1.
21. TB *Berakhot* 28b.
22. TB *Megillah* 17b–18a.
23. Ibid.
24. TB *Berakhot* 5a.
25. TB *Ketubot* 112a.
26. TB *Pesahim* 87b.
27. *Netzah Yisrael.*
28. Rabbi Jacob Emden in the Introduction to the Prayerbook edited by him.
29. TB *Yoma* 9b.
30. *Yisrael veHa'Amim* (Israel and the Nations), p. 182.
31. TB *Kethuboth* 111a and, with some variations in the midrash *Shir Hashirim Rabbah* 2,7.
32. As quoted from the Hebrew pamphlet "Open Up Your Eyes," cited by Rabbi Israel Szczipinski, "Torat Ha-Geula" (The Doctrine of Redemption), in *Torah uMelukhah* (Torah and Sovereignty), Sh. Federbush, ed. (Jerusalem, 1961).
33. Judah Halevi, *Book of the Kuzari,* Hartwig Hirschfeld trans. and annot. (London: M.L. Cailingold, 1931), republished (New York: Pardes, 1961), II, 23.
34. Ibid.
35. Ibid., 29–30.

Israel and Christian Self-Understanding

Br. Marcel J. Dubois

I
ISRAEL AND THE CHRISTIAN CONSCIENCE

It is a fact that the Christian conscience, which has been challenged by the tragedy of the concentration camps and of the Holocaust, received a new stimulus by the creation of the state of Israel.

The ingathering of the children of Israel in the land of the Bible has obliged Christians to become aware of Jewish identity. From now on, Israel has a territory, a flag, a passport, a government, and institutions. The Six-Day War made Christians even more aware of these facts, and this awareness is ever on the increase among attentive Christians who witness Israel's daily struggle for the defense and vindication of its right to exist. It has been reinforced in a tragic way, since the Yom Kippur War, by Israel's isolation among the nations, exemplified by the resolution condemning Zionism as racism, adopted by the General Assembly of the United Nations.

Faced with this new situation, Christians have reacted in different ways.

We all know Jewish friends, and even certain Christians, who proclaim their indifference to Christian reactions on this matter, which for them concerns uniquely and exclusively the Jews. Nevertheless, a Christian who seeks to know and encounter the Jewish reality in its fullness cannot feel unconcerned by the existence of the state of Israel, by the testimony it can bear to Jewish existence with its problems, hopes, and difficulties.

I would simply like to draw up a summary balance sheet of Christian

63

reactions with regard to Israel's return to its land, considering the recent evolution of attitudes and recalling some of the conditions required for a dialogue on this central subject between Jews and Christians.

It is clear that the existence of Israel has had a direct impact on the encounter between Jews and Christians; but we can also be naive and pretentious enough to believe that progress in the dialogue and mutual understanding between Jews and Christians can have a positive—and perhaps demanding—influence on Israeli reality, its comportment, or the way in which it is recognized and accepted in the world.

Major Trends in Recent Christian Theology

Unfortunately, concerning Israel we are too often confronted with simplistic theology. This is the case when we hear the unqualified affirmation that the state of Israel is the unequivocal fulfillment of the biblical prophecies concerning the Jewish people, but no less so when theological arguments are used in denying the right of the Jews to independent national existence in the land of their forefathers.

On one side, the reference to the Bible is sometimes too one-sided, and its application to Israeli reality can become paradoxically dangerous. The late Yona Malachi did very interesting research about the evolution of the feelings of those people who initially justified Zionism because they read in the Bible that the return to Zion is a normal fulfillment of Jewish existence, the accomplishment of the design of God. But since they based their conviction on a very fundamentalist reading of the scripture, they thought they were allowed to judge the behavior of the state of Israel according to their own criteria. Subsequently they became anti-Zionists, because Israel did not behave according to the model they found in the Bible.

On the other side, the trends of a more traditional approach seem to have become more narrow than ever: lack of comprehension and inability to accept the facts. This virtual allergy derives from more or less conscious theological assumptions.

It is strange, but nevertheless true, when Judaism and Israel are in question, that some of the most conservative theologians and the theorists of the new left find themselves in the same camp. It is striking to see many Christian thinkers, belonging either to the right or to the left, with a common allergy to Judaism, deriving from theological positions or assumptions whose only excuse is that they are more or less unconscious.

Many Christians regard Israel as a purely political and secular reality.

As a result, they are unwilling to recognize any link whatsoever between that contemporary reality and the "old" Israel. Victims of a kind of inhibition, the theologians who defend this position fear that doctrinal or scriptural considerations may be used to justify Israel's political existence. Actually, by a curious contradiction, their theology of Israel succeeds in eliminating any theological outlook when the question of the state of Israel is raised.

Their thesis is usually presented according to the traditional argument for the so-called "substitution." According to this view, it was the ordained role of Jewry to prepare the people of God, namely the church. Now that the messiah has come, the church—*verus Israel*—has taken the place of the "old" Israel and the Jewish people no longer has any reason to exist, the Jews as a nation may now vanish and, in any case, have no right to occupy the historic land of Israel. In this way of thinking, another element shows traces of a certain traditional theology. For in this refusal to allow room for a theological consideration of Israel, one can in fact discern a consequence of the old theory of rejection, according to which, in the Christian economy, no theological value whatsoever can be attributed to the Jewish people after the advent of Jesus.

It seems, too, that there is a residue of the deicide myth, implying that the chastisement of Israel is the inability for the Jewish people to ever return to its land. It is quite clear that a Christian can no longer accept this accusation of deicide, but one may ask if a shadow of it does not still survive in the Christian subconscious. Could this shadow explain that indefinable discomfort felt by some Christians at the thought that the holy land, and Jerusalem in particular, are in the hands of the Jews? The general tendency of such a position is roughly that the diaspora is considered to be a consequence of the crucifixion, a punishment for deicide, and that Zionism must therefore be regarded as an arrogant presumption, in opposition to the will of God, who has punished his people and condemned them to exile and wandering. Most distressingly, such Christians believe they can cite the support and authority of the Church fathers, whereas in many cases they project their own antisemitism onto the patristic texts.

These arguments, generally dressed up in theological garb, are too often activated by political considerations and are thus to be found among the slogans of those Christians who belong to the new left. Actually, such a political position is characteristic of a vast movement in which passionate fervor, often generosity, takes precedence over objectivity and clear thinking. Here the theology of anti-Zionism enters into the more general context of a theology of revolution, whether it be called theology of hope, or theology of violence, which is elaborated by Christian political leaders to validate the struggle for justice and the defense of the downtrodden. The impact of this theology on the Christian attitude toward the state of Israel is all the more manifest in that it is, in fact, a matter of justifying and promoting the rights of the Palestinians, who are used as the symbol for the cause of all who are oppressed and exploited, whether they be proletarian classes or underdeveloped countries. Thenceforth, in this simplistic Manicheism, Israel figures as the negative and baleful counterpart. The meetings of the "World Congress of Christians for Palestine" at Beirut in 1970, and at Canterbury in 1972, were the clearest expression of this confusion of planes, in which, on the pretext of defending the Palestinian cause, theological reflection on Israel's existence is denied, while a medley of politics and theology hostile to Israel is in fact elaborated. Since then, reiterated condemnations of Zionism by various international bodies have led to many other elaborations on the same thesis, in which prejudice evidently gets the better of both objectivity and logic.

Sometimes, in order to avoid the accusation of antisemitism, it is asserted that one dissociates Zionism from Judaism, wanting to save the latter at the price of the former. One makes a show of great respect for Jewish identity, trying to point out that it in no way includes the return of the Jews to Zion. A new aspect of the classic caricature of an antisemite saying that his best friends are Jews! In the remarkable report which he elaborated for the meeting of the International Liaison Committee in Jerusalem in March 1976, Rabbi Henry Siegman gave an evaluation, rather cruel but objectively true, of such a position as seen from the Jewish side: "Ironically, it is those who deny the possibility of Jewish nationalism who in fact introduce insupportable and irrelevant theological considerations. It is a phenomenon that brings the Christian right and the Christian left into strange fellowship. Opposition to Israel from the Christian right has the advantage of familiarity and requires no elaboration. The opposition from the left is a more recent phenomenon: their hostility is a peculiar blend of an uncritical celebration of the third world and a theological antisemitism that is nourished by a Christian universalism which cannot abide the earthiness of Jewish particularity. Daniel Berrigan is a good example of those, on the Christian left, who love Jews as disincarnate, suffering servants, ghostly emissaries and symbols of an obscure mission. They cannot abide Jews who are flesh-and-blood people, who are men like other men in all their angularities and particularities, who need to occupy physical space in a real world to fulfill whatever aspirations they may have. They are distressed by the notion that Jews should want a flesh-and-blood existence as a people in the real geography of this world."

Prejudices from the Past

It is only too clear that, in spite of all their differences, both the traditional and the new left theologies have inherited the prejudices of that ancient anti-Judaism based on a collection of affirmations formulated during the bitter period of the implacable separation of church and synagogue. According to the spirit of these affirmations, Judaism was considered only as a preparation for the gospel and nothing more, as something destined to vanish with the advent of the redeemer, as a faith that was decadent and legalistic—in the time of Jesus at least—and, after his coming, as a faith decrepit and emptied of all spiritual substance, a religion destined to survive only, according to Augustine's famous formula, as "a witness of the church's truth and of the Jews' iniquity."

It can be said that many of these affirmations manifest the permanence of a certain Marcionism in Christian thought. The second century heretic Marcion rejected the Old Testament as the word of the demiurge and not the word of God, emphasizing in a radical way the break between the Jewish people and the true people of God. Though condemned by the church, it must be said that Marcionism remained as a permanent temptation. There is no doubt that it is more or less implicit in the theological tendency that radically de-Judaizes the church, reducing the Old Testament to nothing more than a simple manual of pious thoughts. By a purely allegorical interpretation, it does in fact sever the church from its historical and existential roots. All this has obviously weakened faith, both in the very consistency of biblical history and its divine significance, and in the conviction that God can still act magnanimously in history—including the specific history of the people of the Bible—as he did of old.

The same oblique notion affects the usage made of typology in traditional exegesis and theology. Manipulated to delineate the stages of God's design, typology proposes a marvelous key of intelligibility for understanding the continuity and progress of the history of salvation. In this perspective, the Old Testament is the prophecy and the sacrament of the New Testament. The destiny of Israel announces, prepares, and signifies the destination of the church.

However, when typology plays with the opposition between the past and the present, as the opposition between the symbol and the reality, its univocal application is fraught with dangers one has not always been on guard against.

The first of these dangers is that of some form of Platonism, that is to say a hasty spiritualism, avoidable only with difficulty as soon as one opposes sign and reality. In fact, the risk is to insist so much on signified reality that one comes to neglect, if not to suppress, the consistency of the sign. If the significance of terrestrial Jerusalem is only to herald celestial Jerusalem, what can be her destination, from the moment one believes that reality is accomplished?

Then the second danger is to fall into a pessimistic dualism, in which the first term of comparison appears necessarily pejorative. Here, past and present, in the case of Israel and the church, the two are not anymore opposed as the figure and the reality, the announcement and the accomplishment, but as the shadow and the light, the letter and the spirit, the carnal and the spiritual. In this view of things, the Jewish people can only be considered as a reality decidedly terrestrial, obscure, and carnal, when facing a celestial, radiant, and spiritual church, appearing as the realization of God's people.

Such simplifications are all the more dangerous when they risk being used as purely abstract categories. This is the kind of danger one incurs with a typology that is only an algebra of symbols and oppositions, used, so to speak, only for itself, without reference to reality. At the close of such a manipulation of coupled contraries, one comes almost inevitably to a kind of Manichean vision, in which the church is the *verus Israel* and the authentic Jerusalem, and in which, then, the people of the Bible and the earthly Jerusalem are set aside with Babylon.

In their usage of typology, at least at the level of literary expression and symbolics, the church fathers did not always escape these dangers. In utilizing terms from the epistle to the Hebrews (8:5; 9:23; 10:1), one can say that, as much in their comprehension of Israel and of the Jewish people as in their conception of the relationship between the Old and the New Testaments, they never ceased to oscillate between two visions of things, insisting sometimes on the shadow and sometimes on the figure, sometimes on the rupture and sometimes on the continuity.

One easily sees the danger of a unilateral and univocal insistence on such an opposition in terms of contrariety. For a typology which holds to this aspect of things only, the people of Israel loses all consistency, in any case all positive consistency. Not only the symbol disappears before the reality it was proclaiming, but its existence itself, carnal, terrestrial, dark, becomes decidedly pejorative. At the limit, one reaches the paradox of a sacrament without matter. Israel is the type of the church, but does not exist anymore by itself. The terrestrial Jerusalem is the sacrament of the celestial Jerusalem, but her human and terrestrial realization is in some way put within brackets. And the link between the Jewish people and the land was only a temporal concession, temporary and now revoked.

But despite the abstract typology, the Jewish people persists in its existence, in its national conscience, and at the same time in its religious fidelity. Moreover, it asserts its link with the land where it had lived its destiny at the time of the Bible! The above reflections show that the framework, and sometimes the clichés, of a certain traditional theology, whether they come from the right or the left, are not capable of explaining this state of things.

In the report already cited—articulating the Jewish position in response to those Christians who refuse to recognize in the state of Israel any theological implications, or to those who try to dissociate, in speaking of Jews and Israel, the religious and political dimensions—Rabbi Henry Siegman proposes a justification to which both Christians and Jews must pay attention, because it stems from the roots of a very deep tradition: "The truth of the matter," he says, "is that Israel presents not only a political issue, but has the profoundest theological implications, and these go to the very heart of the Christian-Jewish encounter. It may be Jews who have returned to Tel Aviv, but Judaism that has returned to Jerusalem."

Here lies the difficulty inherent in all considerations of Judaism and of the Jewish condition. This condition is complex; its components are easily discernible, but its concrete synthesis is so deep that it is difficult to see them in a simple unity. This is certainly one of the reasons why the Jews find it so hard to define themselves. Judaism comprises two inseparable elements: a nation whose vocation is religious, a religion whose basis is national. The entire history of the Jewish people could be summarized in the history of its oscillations between these two poles: secular and sacred; political and religious; historical and mystical; and we could add here: immanent and transcendent, particular and universal.

The creation of the state of Israel, far from simplifying this complexity, has increased it. Zionism was certainly, at the beginning, a nationalist movement with secular and even areligious origins, yet it has found its most precious sources, its creative dynamism, in the vitality of religious tradition and in the fervor of the lovers of Zion. It must not be concluded from this that the state of Israel finds the energy of its will-to-live in a religious chauvinism or exclusiveness.

If Christians feel so ill at ease in interpreting the peculiar brand of

Israeli nationalism, it is because they are not yet capable of accommodating in their faith the complex elements which, for the Jewish consciousness, are absolutely fundamental. Election and the Jewish people's link with the land are, without any doubt, the most important of these. What remains of the ancient promises now that Christ has come? What is the value now of seeking to justify, from the Bible or religious tradition, the link between the Jewish people and the land promised to it long ago? Plainly, Christian theology has not yet found a complete and satisfactory answer to these questions.

For the Jewish conscience, even if these elements are not clearly situated and recognized, Israel's election and its link with the land are absolutely vital realities. If Christians wish to understand the Jewish destiny, the return to Zion, and the attitude of the Israelis, they must at least take into consideration the traditional inspiration of this national sentiment, connecting it with its sources, respecting it as felt from within.

It seems to me that a new Christian theology is emerging which is consonant with this attitude of respect for Jewish self-understanding.

Signs of Renewal, Dynamics of Reevaluation

We can observe nowadays, in certain Christian circles, a more open attitude, one more respectful of reality—that of Christians with a knowledge of Israel's past and history and conscious of the permanence of God's plan, who study the modern history of the Jews within the general perspective of the history of salvation. In this great adventure of Israel from Abraham to the present day, they discover the continuity of a divine teaching with regard to a people that remains mysteriously marked by its original election.

It would be interesting to analyze, step by step, the progress which has been made during the last decades. As signs of this positive development, I could quote here many documents and testimonies, from both the top and the bottom of Christian hierarchies and communities. The work of theological reflection undertaken in Jewish-Christian circles has, in many ways, prepared the elaboration of official documents emanating from various church authorities, and those documents have, reciprocally, stimulated the process of theological thinking and encouraged Christian encounter with the Jewish reality.

Whatever the content of these documents, with the definite novelty of their approach and their issues, it seems to me that the very dynamism of their inspiration, as manifested in their progressive development, is, in itself, full of significance. We have to pay attention to this dynamism, this inside movement, to this increasing openness of Christian thought to Jewish values and subjectivity.

From this point of view, for instance, we can say that the importance of the Second Vatican Council for relations between Jews and Christians, and for the church's attitude toward Israel, will emerge more and more clearly with time. Evaluating the significance of this text, a few years after the council, Father Edward H. Flannery had no hesitation in observing: "If Israel's participation in the election and covenant is still valid for the Jewish people, the covenant and promise should be understood in their original meaning. . . . They should, in other words, include Israel as a land. The burden of proof seems to rest on him who holds that Israel's continuing covenant must be a landless one. Admittedly, this theological reclamation of the land revolutionizes the traditional Christian conception of Judaism. But so does the Vatican Council's statement on the Jewish people in other equally important respects. Then, too, the repossession of Palestine by Jews in our time is of a magnitude which invites revision of much thinking, secular as well as religious."

In this dynamic perspective, the text published by the Committee of the French Bishops, on the eve of Passover 1973, represents progress with regard to former theological positions. The principal import of this document is a pressing demand made upon the Christian conscience for the discovery in its own self-image of features received from its Jewish roots.

This is far less a question of purely theoretical study than of a discovery which concerns the very progress of Christian life: "Christians, even if only for their own sake, must acquire a true and living knowledge of the Jewish tradition." Much more, the text wishes that "all Christians . . . seek to understand the Jew as he understands himself, instead of judging him according to their own way of thinking." So the Jews are no longer a pure object and Judaism a theological issue. Christians are asked to discover Jewish subjectivity from within.

Of particular importance is what is meant here by "Jewish existence." It is, of course, a question of "the actual existence of the Jewish people" but also "its precarious condition throughout its history, its hope, the tragedies which it has known in the past and, above all in modern time, its partial ingathering in the land of the Bible." A little further, the text speaks of "its search for its identity among other men, its constant effort to gather together in a reunified community."

Yet a complete and attentive reading of the text shows a determination for justice and equilibrium which forbids any simplistic or unilateral interpretation. Certainly it is clearly affirmed: "Beyond the legitimate diversity of political options, the universal conscience cannot refuse to the Jewish people, which has undergone so many vicissitudes in the course of its history, the right and the means for a political existence among the nations." However, it is evident that Israel is not mentioned as a state and that Zionism is not named. Above all, the authors of the text are very conscious of the extreme complexity of the problem and wish to place the document in its full context: "It is, at the present time, harder than ever to make a serene theological judgment on the movement of the Jewish people for a return to 'its' land."

Bearing this in mind, it is easy to discern the real intention of the document. The French bishops ask their faithful to become aware of what a return to Jerusalem means to the Jewish spirit, and to question themselves about the significance of this new ingathering: "In the presence of this return, we cannot, as Christians, forget the gift formerly made to the people of Israel of a land in which it was called to be reunited." Henceforward, Christians "must take account of the interpretation given to their regathering around Jerusalem by the Jews who, in the name of their faith, consider it a blessing."

Compared with this hopeful and generous invitation to Christian conscience, the "Guidelines" published by the Vatican Commission at the beginning of 1975 have appeared to many readers and to our Jewish friends in particular as a halt or even as a step backward. Such was, for instance, the reaction of Henry Siegman in the report quoted above. In spite of his deep friendship for the authors of this document, he wrote: "The failure of the Vatican Guidelines to deal with the theological dimension of the Jewish relationship to the land constituted a grievous omission. Within the context of the document's own declared desire to understand Jews as they understand themselves, it must be faulted for failing to spell out to Catholics that . . . it is impossible to understand Jews, nor can anyone communicate meaningfully with them about their fears and aspirations, without an appreciation of the role of the state of Israel in Jewish consciousness."

We can share, or at least understand, this disappointment. But, without trying to play here the role of devil's advocate, I am convinced that, as I said before, the development of theological thinking, the dynamism of the process which brings this text, is, in some way, more important than the details of its contents. In requiring Christians to strive to learn "by what essential traits the Jews define themselves in the light of their own religious experience," the Vatican Guidelines have definitely adopted a very important principle.

A New Approach to Judaism and to Israeli Reality

At the present stage of this reevaluation it can be said that, at a more rigorously theological level, the least apparent but most decisive, many Christians are beginning to ask themselves questions, in a clearer and more urgent way, about the significance of Judaism and the destiny of Israel.

Of course, the theology about these questions is still under research. Ways of expressing such a difficult and essential reality more adequately are still sadly lacking. Fortunately, however, some Christians, without yet being capable of defining their convictions with reasons and words, are beginning to sense that it is impossible to understand, justly and truthfully, the present situation in the Middle East without recognizing the peculiarity of the Jewish people, with all that this implies: its permanence through time, its spiritual tradition, its historical dynamism, the continuity of its religious and national conscience, the living link of the people with the Bible and with its land.

From this point of view, one may say that the recognition of the state of Israel assumes the multiple and unpredictable form of contacts between Christians and Israelis. These contacts are established at the level not of institutions and principles, but of everyday life. More and more Christians come to Israel in order to explore all its aspects, work in kibbutzim, or study at the Hebrew University. Moreover, Jewish and Christian intellectuals meet in study groups for common research and true dialogue.

To be sure, these people are still isolated cases, often ignored by the authorities, and sometimes even feared or regarded as unrepresentative individuals. Often these Christians are, indeed, still pioneers; but their presence and their contacts with Israeli friends are a new facet of the relationship between the churches and the state of Israel, full of promise for the future.

This is another way of recognizing that the existence and the behavior of the state of Israel, as with the Jewish condition and the present situation of Judaism, can be judged only if the subjectivity of the Jewish soul is respected, as it were, from within. The complexity and the convergence of all the components of Judaism—faith, history, tradition, messianic hope, national will-to-live—cannot be forgotten since, here in this country, they are always present simultaneously.

The existence of Israel, that is to say, the assembling of the Jewish people in a land of their own, in which they can live in accordance with their tradition, gives Christians the paradoxical advantage—radically now as regards the encounter with Judaism—of being a minority. Our experience here is the same as that of the Jews during centuries in the midst of the Christian nations. Our communities here are stripped of all imperialism or colonialism, whether doctrinal or juridical. Such a situation is very healthy, for on the one hand our Jewish friends no longer feel they are strangers or threatened in their identity, whereas we encounter them without the protection of false securities. Thus the encounter becomes more true, devoid of fear and illusion, with a great exigency of authenticity.

Innumerable are the advantages of such a climate for a mutual discovery and a mutual understanding. I will only mention one of these experiences which seems to me the most important: the discovery of the synchrony which unites the land, the landscapes and significant places of this land, the Bible, and the people living here. Living in Jerusalem, all the details of daily existence direct our attention to the significance, for Jews, of the holy land and of this city. *Torat Yisrael, Eretz Yisrael, Am Yisrael* —Bible, land, and people—linked in a covenantal bond that is everlasting.

As a matter of fact, there is an increasing flow of pilgrims of a new kind. They come to Jerusalem because they have discovered the importance of this city to their understanding of the word of God and the centrality of this city in the whole history of salvation. There are more and more scholars, clergymen, and students who come to Israel to read the Bible on the spot, to rediscover the roots of their faith. We could summarize the process of this movement using the three words we have just recalled, which express the pillars of Jewish identity: *Torah, Am, Aretz;* the Bible, the people, and the land. First, they come to Jerusalem to realize the link between the Bible and the land. Second, they come to take advantage of the Jewish approach to the Bible in order to renew their own reading of the scripture: the people and the Bible. At the end of the process, they become more aware of the link between the people and this land.

SHARING THE EXPERIENCE OF THE JEWISH PEOPLE: UNIQUENESS AND EXEMPLARITY

An honest balance sheet would acknowledge that considerable progress has been made in the discovery of our common roots and of the continuity of the destiny which links us. Christians have given more and deeper consideration to the exemplarity of the Hebrew Bible, which we call the Old Testament, and to the dynamism of God's design in the history of salvation. We shall never insist enough on the fact that the Bible and the people whose spiritual adventure is recounted in it have a value at once unique and exemplary. Unique, because it is the singular account of the singular history of a particular people. Exemplary, because this singularity is open to the universal. Everyone can find his own story in the dialogue of this people with its God, who is also the God of us Christians, since he is the God of Jesus Christ.

Jewish Heritage in Christian Existential Behavior

In this perspective, a Christian reflecting on Jewish reality—especially if he lives in Israel among the Jewish people regathered in the land of the Bible—is soon amazed to discover that the heritage he shares with the Jews does not consist only in a book that can be read objectively, nor in a store of truths whose contents it suffices to learn and analyze. This heritage involves the very attitude of Israel before its gifts and their giver, the very manner in which this people has received this book, preserved and transmitted it.

If I had to explain to somebody who does not share my faith—a Marxist, a Buddhist, or an atheist—not so much the contents of my creed, but more precisely the characteristics of my spiritual attitude, the existential dimensions of my Christian behavior, I would do it in the way of a croquis of Matisse, with six simple features. As a Christian, I *listen* to God speaking, so faith is an act of hearing; as a Christian, I *remember,* I recall in my living memory the words and deeds of the one who has spoken; as a Christian, I do not do that alone, I *participate in a community* of brothers and sisters who listen and remember as I do; together with them I *record* what God has said and done in a permanent tradition; on the basis of this tradition, and together with these sisters and brothers, I *thank God,* I sing and praise for the sanctification of the name; finally, as a Christian, I *hope* for, I am expecting the coming or the return of the one who has spoken and has promised his advent.

Unfortunately, we are not enough aware of these features which constitute our Christian identity, and still much less of the original source of this likeness. Too often we forget that the fundamental characteristics of the Christian attitude in the presence of the God who created and spoke to man—the *hearing* of his word, the *memory* of its challenge and of the one who speaks it, the *tradition* which preserves and transmits this memory, the *community* this tradition gathers, the song of praise and *thanksgiving* of this community, and finally the *hope* founded on this hearing and memory—are all a heritage which we have received from the Jewish people. It is not merely a content but a comportment, not only a message but a living relation with the one who speaks. *Shema Yisrael,* or "Hear, Israel." We are the heirs of an invitation to attention, and to the fundamental dependence implied in it. As a matter of fact, only a witness to this memory and hope, one which expresses Israel's relationship to its God, the creature's to the creator, man's to the one who saves him, can inspire the message which this tottering world is more or less consciously seeking in response to the crises and questions of our modern age.

A Christian philosopher of our time has defined hope as "the memory of the future." He unwittingly paraphrases the statement of the Baal Shem Tov: *Zikaron Petach ha-Ge'ulah,* "Memory is the gateway to redemption." And it is the Christian in Solzhenitsyn who speaks when he tells the western world carried away by the novelty of its inventions and discoveries: "A people which has no memory has no future!"

"Memory of the future": this definition expresses accurately the attitude which joins the Jewish people and the church in the memory and mystery of time. Saint Augustine expresses the same perception in a formulation open to the depths of self-consciousness: "*Meminisse sui, meminisse Dei.*" To remember the self is to remember God in the self. Beneath every act in which I perceive myself in my particular, unique, and incommunicable identity, I can intuit the source who inexhaustibly gives me my existence and my name. "I and my creator," as Cardinal Newman said. Through my memory, I meet the one who created me, the one who in pronouncing the word which defines me called me into being. This is why memory is also the faculty of the future, because the word which calls me into being is at the same time vocation and promise. The future is inscribed in being as God created it and sees it at each instant. The present is rich with promise of a destiny carried by God in his plan. This plan carries, in its own dynamism, the possibility for being which corresponds to God's dream for me. The one who calls me by name is also the one who attracts me and awaits me. To hope is precisely to believe in this care that God has for everything, for the universe, for me. It is to have confidence in his attentive care which embraces the present, the future and eternity. It is to believe in the potential for being inscribed in present reality. This is the sense in which hope can be called "memory of the future."

Each of us can discover this confidence, this touchstone of faith, in the act of remembering self; and what is true for all persons and destinies is also true for the people of God as a whole. Moreover, one can say that the history of the people of God is the image and example of this memory of the future. Throughout the Bible, the people of Israel is sustained by a word which is at once call and promise. From the beginning, the word of God to Abraham and Moses proclaims a design and announces a plenitude. The secret of the dynamism of the Jewish people, and the enduring source of its fidelity and persistence, has always been its active memory of what has been announced as future fulfillment. The secret of the church's development throughout the centuries that span Christ's coming and return is of the same nature. Yesterday, today, and tomorrow, the Lord is alive. It is one and the same movement that announces his return and leaves us the memorial of his presence. "Do this in memory of me." "You proclaim the death of the Lord until He comes." To hope is at the same time to be certain of his coming and to believe that the promised future is already at work in the present.

Such confidence in the future is founded definitively on God's own memory. For it is he whose presence endures, and it is he who remembers. The psalms refer to this memory of God "recalling his love and fidelity for the house of Israel" (98:3). And Mary expresses thanks for this memory of the Lord who realizes his promises: "He remembers his mercy which he has promised to Abraham and to his seed forever" (Lk 1:54–55). We see that, in the presence of God, Jews and Christians are united in the same fundamental attitude, inspired by the same Spirit, coming from the same original source. It suffices to recall here Martin Buber's reflections on the "I and Thou" to understand that God is the only one to whom I can truly say "thou," the only one who is himself truly "I," the "I" which is the source of the "I" that I am, with my autonomy and dependence. Such is certainly the meaning of this expression of our common tradition: "Avinu Malkeinu"—Our Father, our king.

The Election and the Solitude of Israel

Let us reflect on the nature of election, on its consequences for the Jewish soul and destiny, and also on what I call the reverse of election, that is to say, the paradoxical solitude into which Israel is led by the election. A Christian should admire, and rejoice over, the singularity which is the consequence of election. Far from being a vocation shut up in itself, it is a model for all spiritual adventure. It is an exemplary destiny opened to universality. Let us consider first the positive aspect of things, the privileged—should one say aristocratic?—solitude into which the election introduces Israel. In order to understand its wealth, it is sufficient to recall three initial facts which condition the very essence of Judaism.

There is, in the first place, the fact that the Bible, in spite of its universal destination, is at the outset the history of a particular people and that it addresses itself first to this people. The Jews listen to it, receive it, transmit it as the word of God to Israel. This gives to the Jewish reading of the Bible a realism and an urgency, where the consciousness of election manifests itself in action: ethnocentrism and theocentrism at the same time.

The second fact that impresses me is that the original affirmation of the medieval Jewish philosophers is not "God is" or "God is the cause," but "God gave the Torah to this people on Mount Sinai": a certitude obtained at the same time by faith and by the consciousness of belonging to a people that knows that God spoke. This word, this message, consists less of the teaching of a doctrine than of the proposition of a way of life which sets a people apart. God speaks: "*Shema Yisrael*," "Hear, Israel"; he calls, he proposes to his people an answer which assumes the form of a way of life whose details are determined by the *mitzvot,* the observance of the commandments. The Torah unifies the people through the same calling and the same answer. It sets the people apart from the other nations, because it introduces the solitude of a particular way of life.

Third, the manner in which the Jews have kept the treasure of their tradition has also been a factor setting them apart. Gripped by this "estrangement," we Gentiles have shut them up in the ghetto, but they, in order to fiercely guard their identity, had already followed the counsel of their sages and "built a fence around the Torah."

These three traits would be sufficient to show that it is a question, above all, of a positive solitude—a solitude which, on God's side, results from the choice itself, and which is maintained, on the side of the people, in the consciousness of chosenness. To retain Jewish identity is, at the same time, to keep to the true God, to keep to the tradition, and to keep to the cohesion of the people chosen by God.

Seen from the outside, this consciousness of being chosen can appear as a self-segregation and an intolerance. Indeed, it is this determined particularity which, while preserving the Jewish identity, has upheld in this world the absolute faith in the one God. We inherited the benefit of that intolerance which the Jews exhibited toward paganism throughout the centuries.

Paul Claudel perceived admirably both aspects of this intransigent solitude—on the one hand, the refusal of the world, in the name of the ineluctable preference for Jerusalem: "since the world organizes itself for a certain refusal of God, it is he (Israel) who shall be the refusal of the refusal;" and on the other hand, the fact that in this world all solitude on behalf of God condemns man to an inevitable isolation: "it is not surprising that we disturb society and that, after some time, society does not resist the desire to throw us out: we do not belong."

A Christian cannot but respect this singular solitude. How can we not feel invited to attention, as before the trace of a destiny? It is strange that this Jewish singularity has been so badly understood and has been so often the occasion of hostility and scorn. Maybe it is because one has not perceived that the election introduces the Jewish people to a destiny which—unique and singular as it is—is at the same time universal and exemplary.

Singularity in view of exemplariness. This being true of Jewish history as a whole, the experience of the Holocaust constituted an altogether particular application. The horrible and tragic character of this event is also absolutely unique; but considered in the light of a history marked by election, it too becomes rich with exemplary significance and of universal application.

The sufferings of Israel, like its destiny, have an exemplary value for all human sufferings. It is in fact, for the Jewish people, a consequence of the mystery of the election. This invites the Jewish soul to see in every distress and every misfortune of this world a meaning in the light of its own experience.

Jewish tradition has recognized in Israel's grievous destiny—both singular and mysterious—a value for the salvation of the world. In the darkness of its history Israel has recognized its own image in the features of the mysterious figure of the suffering servant of the Lord described in Isaiah. Faced with the exemplariness of the Holocaust with regard to all human suffering and the mystery of death, and with the exemplary redeeming value of the suffering of Israel, the Christian feels himself invited to meditation and silence. How could he not feel himself questioned by a mystery so similar and so near to that which is at the heart of his faith?

This paradox of singularity and universality, which is given with election, comes to very topical and contemporary expression in the return of the Jews to Zion.

III
LIVING IN JERUSALEM

The link of the people of Israel with Jerusalem, its place at the center of Jewish identity, involves very demanding requirements. Since the mystery which is at the center of Christian faith took place in Jerusalem, there is also an original and essential link between this city and Christian identity. Whatever the differences between the two links and the two approaches, Jews and Christians are connected to Jerusalem in ways which concern their self-understanding. In the depth of their vocation to righteousness and sanctity, both of them are confronted with the fundamental paradox of a city which is at the same time a sign of contradiction and a pole of unity.

The Meaning of Jerusalem in Jewish Identity

The relationship which binds the Jewish people to Jerusalem could be summarized by these three words: centrality, sacramentality, and universality.

Centrality, because Jerusalem is at the center of Jewish prayer, Jewish observance, Jewish existence—just as it has been the object of Jewish nostalgia for centuries.

Sacramentality, because, for a Jew, Jerusalem is simultaneously a mystery and a reality. This city—*Yerushalayim shel zahav*—the golden Jerusalem, is not only the symbol of a celestial city, the heavenly Jerusalem, but an earthly city of human beings, the city of which Teddy Kollek is mayor. It is simultaneously the political capital of this nation and the site of the Temple, over which the *Shekhinah* remains present; the historical setting of battles for eternal realities; a home and a sanctuary; a city where the profane and the sacred, the human and the divine, history and eternity are interwoven.

Universality, because the vocation of this city is that of being both definitely singular—it is a Jewish city—and yet open to the whole world; a sanctuary, given to the Jews, but to which all nations are invited to come.

Thus, in God's education of his people, as we find it in the Bible and as the Jews understand it, the return to Zion appears as a preliminary phase and the symbol of a much greater reality than the reconquest of a capital; it is a sacrament of the conversion of the heart, the challenging revelation of a call to peace and a universal presence of which Jerusalem is the center.

Unhappily, this vision, inspired by Isaiah and the other prophets, may seem very far from day-to-day reality, from the tumult of conflicts and threats of war. Yet through this reality we can see how the Jewish consciousness in Israel is irresistibly drawn to awareness of its true role and destiny as it seeks to be faithful to itself. It is in this light that we must look at Israel and invite it to evaluate itself, with the patience of God.

Several times since the Six-Day War, Israeli audiences—university students, kibbutzniks, army officers—have asked me what I, as a Christian living here, think of the destiny of Israel as attested by its recent history: *galut* and *geulah,* the exile and redemption of the Jewish people, dispersion and return to Zion: how should one interpret these? It was in the message of Isaiah that I found the substance of my reply. To Israeli friends I answered:

"Your return to Jerusalem has significance only if you understand and accept all its challenges. To come back to Jerusalem is not only, for the Jewish people, a matter of regaining the political capital of a nation which has finally acquired its territory and independence. To come back to Jerusalem, for the Jewish soul, means to assume the spiritual responsibility of a vocation which concerns the entire universe, its unity, its harmony and peace.

"What does this universal vocation consist of? What are its promises and its demands? You know that, as a Christian, I have my own answers. But you, children of Israel, in the sincerity of your Jewish conscience, must recognize yours. Return to Zion, return to God. For a Jewish soul, these two movements cannot be dissociated. I, as a Christian, invite you to recognize the challenge in this. It is an awesome responsibility, and a mysterious destiny: no one knows where it will lead and what it will demand, if you are to be true to yourselves. This is the price you must pay, if the will-to-live of the Jewish people is to have vindication and meaning."

I know that such language may be misunderstood by realists and

extremists in both camps: inveterate anti-Zionists and unconditional nationalists. It seems, however, to be the only way to achieve mutual respect
and bring about peace in the long run.

If we believe in the continuity of the divine plan, of which this people
was bearer and first messenger, it seems more consistent with biblical and
gospel logic to trust in the dynamism of God's gift.

This is what is demanded of us Christians if we are to have the right to
judge and speak truthfully. Respecting the self-awareness of the Jewish
soul and espousing that dynamic force which sets its most vital pleas in
motion, we will perhaps be able to grasp the real significance of this dynamism, to manifest the responsibility which it implies, even to purify it and
guide it in the context of a fraternal, true, yet demanding confrontation
with our Israeli friends.

Israel received the gift of Jerusalem, which involves an immense
responsibility before God and before the world. This requires from Israel a
twofold step, and, at the limit, a twofold generosity of selflessness. First,
back in its city, the Jewish people is called to say to all the world: "I have
received and I guard Jerusalem, but I know that this city does not belong
to me alone. I am conscious that I am only the depository. I have received
Jerusalem, and I am ready to give it to the world and to share it with all
people of good will."

Israel certainly does that. The mayor of Jerusalem, Teddy Kollek,
would say with reason: "But such is precisely the situation. Never has
Jerusalem been so well-kept, nor so wide open. Look at the crowds which
come and intermingle here, coming from all the horizons of the world.
Never has Jerusalem realized so well its vocation to universality."

But the Jewish people is invited, in accordance with its vocation, to
go even farther. Israel is asked to recognize the gratuitousness of the gift, at
the very moment lifting it up and showing it to the world, and to say: "I
have received it and I share the gift which was made to me," invalidating,
so to speak, from the inside, the first-person singular. Then it would receive, guard, open and share the gift of God at the same time as a prince
and as a pauper, as a prince because as a pauper, as a prodigal and generous benefactor because everything has been given to him. In this way the
people of the Bible would also, in its present condition, remain a model to
all beneficiaries of God's gifts.

Such is without any doubt the ultimate significance of the return to
Zion and the demand that it implies. It is, in fact, the paradigm for every
act of sanctification. And it would be, for us, very much out of place to
reproach Israel for not having realized it yet. Our task as Christians is,

through love and prayer, to help Israel assume this grand and difficult role in gratitude and humility.

Challenged by Contradictions

In order to understand the authentic meaning of Jerusalem for their faith, Christians who live in this city, or who come to it as pilgrims, are required to overcome another kind of difficulty: the disconcerting paradox of unity and disunity, of identity and contradiction. It is unfortunately true that many Christians are shocked, and even scandalized, when they first visit the holy sepulchre. It is indeed paradoxical that, at the very place where Christ has brought unity and peace to the world through the mystery of his death and resurrection, Christians are themselves in a state of disunity which sometimes results in open conflict. What a contradiction!

There is another place in Jerusalem where the paradox is still more striking: the Cenaculum on Mount Zion. This little fourteenth century Gothic church was built to commemorate two decisive events which are at the very center of the Christian faith: the last supper, during which Jesus instituted the sacrament of the eucharist; and the day of Pentecost, the gift of the Holy Spirit to the apostles and to the early Christian community. At this site, which should be for our faith the concrete memorial of the unity brought to the world by Christ and confirmed by the visit of the Holy Spirit, what do we see today? An empty church, in which official cult and prayer are forbidden because of the "status quo," which was used for centuries as a mosque by Moslems under Turkish rule, and which is today supervised by the Israeli Ministry of Religious Affairs!

If I had to illustrate to a group of Martians visiting our planet just how disunified our world is, I would bring them to the Cenaculum. This place is like an *anti*-sacrament of peace, a sign that harmony and unity don't exist between men who believe in the same unique God! The monotheisms appear at this place, which is for Christians the symbol of unity and peace, in a state of tension and disarray.

And if I had to explain the complexity of the political situation in the Middle East, I would take as an example the differences, and even the divisions, between the Christian churches in Jerusalem. As a matter of fact, they are characterized by three dichotomies which are essentially one. The first dichotomy is between modernity and tradition; tradition in the worst sense of the word: the churches of the Old City are paralyzed by the "status quo." Because of rules and treaties fixed for centuries, they are unable to change anything at the holy places. On the other hand, the Christians in West Jerusalem live as they would in Times Square, Whitechapel or Place Clichy in Paris. They are condemned, so to speak, to modernity, if they want to be in touch with the Jews who live in Israel.

The second dichotomy is that between the churches whose theology is traditionally anti-Judaic, emphasizing the opposition and the rupture between Judaism and Christianity, and those whose members came here precisely in order to establish contact with Judaism, to live among the Jews, and to learn from them elements of Jewish tradition which were forgotten through the centuries.

The third dichotomy—the most superficial yet the most explosive—is the one between the churches whose members are Palestinians and those whose members are Israelis. It is an unavoidable, but painful, one. Only prayer and charity can overcome it. One can understand how difficult it is on the human and political level.

As a matter of fact, these three dichotomies are actually one. This fact must be borne in mind if we are to understand the Christian outlook on Jerusalem. Even as Christians, we are divided by two cultures, two mentalities, two different political approaches—according to two different citizenships.

In spite of the pity of such a situation and of the scandal which it causes, we can nevertheless discover in it a positive significance. The divisions between Churches at the holy sepulchre, and between people of good will at the Cenaculum, are a paradoxical sign of a common longing for unity and peace. This longing is expressed through misunderstandings, confrontations, and conflicts. But in the light of its eternal vocation, as expressed in the Bible, Jerusalem appears as the paradoxical sacrament of our common vocation to harmony and unity, beyond the failures and contradictions of human life in this world.

The Sacramental Meaning of Jerusalem for Christians

If I had to summarize in one word the richness and the ambiguity of the meaning of Jerusalem for Christians, I would use the word "sacramentality," which means, at the same time, both tangible reality and spiritual significance. A sacrament is a sign, a symbol, of a sacred reality, with all the ambivalence and even the ambiguity—the twofold value which comes from the different emphasis either on terrestrial consistency or on spiritual transparency. This is the reason why we can observe in the Christian approach to Jerusalem a kind of oscillation between two frames of reference, worldly realism and heavenly transcendence. Since there is in Jerusalem a permanent unity between time and eternity—*"ha'olam hazeh and ha'olam habah,"* the terrestrial and the celestial, the empirical and the mystical—and because of this original ambivalence, this city is, at the same time, a sign of contradiction and a pole of unity for Christians.

To understand this paradox, I invite you to consider some of its phenomenological manifestations in history. First: What did Jerusalem mean for Jesus? We see in the gospel that it was the center of his life, because he was a Jew. All the greatest events of his life, and especially the events most important for the Christian faith—his passion, his death, and his resurrection—took place in Jerusalem. The holy city was, for him, both the place where dwells the *Shekhinah,* as for every Jew, and the place of his own mystery. Already as a child, and later with his disciples, he came faithfully to Jerusalem on pilgrimage. It was, indeed, the focus of his destiny.

We read in the gospel that when he decided to go to Jerusalem to fulfill his vocation, *"He hardened his face toward Jerusalem."* And we can understand his love for the city from his words (Lk 13:34): *"Jerusalem, Jerusalem, you that kill the prophets and stone those who are sent to you! How often have I longed to gather your children, as a hen gathers her brood under her wings, and you refused!"* This shows, in a rather tragic way, his personal tenderness for Jerusalem.

But, at the same time, we can see that he expresses, in his own person, a radical transposition: He himself is the Temple: *"Destroy this sanctuary and in three days I will raise it up. . . . But he was speaking of the sanctuary that was his body"* (Jn 2:19–21). More precisely, speaking to a woman near Shechem, in Samaria, he explains to her that the Temple and the holy places of this earth are provisional, temporary, relative to another kind of presence: *"Our father worshiped on this mountain (Mount Gerizim), while you say that Jerusalem is the place where one ought to worship.—Jesus said: Believe me, woman, the hour is coming when you will worship the Father, neither on this mountain nor in Jerusalem. . . . But the hour will come, in fact it is here already, when true worshipers will worship the Father in spirit and truth"* (Jn 4:20–23). In other words, the true temple, the true place for the encounter with God, is transcendent and internal: Jerusalem and the Temple are only the physical manifestation or the symbol of a higher and more spiritual reality.

We can observe this same permanent association between terrestrial reality and spiritual significance in the faith and behavior of the early Christian community. For example, we read in the Acts of the Apostles that, immediately after the departure of Christ, Peter and John remained in Jerusalem and behaved as faithful Jews, going regularly to the Temple for worship. Nevertheless, at the same time, we observe a kind of detachment and transposition about the meaning of Jerusalem for Christians. It meant that, from a terrestrial point of view, Jerusalem was no longer a national center for the Christians. For Christians, as such, there is no homeland in this world. The entire earth has become the holy land. For Christianity, Jerusalem remains a spiritual center, the holy place par excellence, but this link with the city does not involve any terrestrial possession or national belonging. After Constantine, when the Roman empire became officially Christian, Jerusalem, with all its holy places, the holy sepulchre in particular, became a spiritual center of devotion and pilgrimage.

In short, throughout history we can see that, despite some aspects of Byzantine rule or of the Latin kingdom, Jerusalem is not a political or even a terrestrial reality at all for Christians. To the Christian faith, this city is, at the same time, both a holy place sanctified by the mystery of salvation which took place in it, and a symbol of another, transcendent and spiritual, reality, the celestial Jerusalem, ultimately the sacrament of the kingdom of God, whose Christ is the Lord.

So we can observe the process of spiritualization of the meaning of Jerusalem which has resulted in the ambiguity, or the ambivalence, of "sacramentality." We have observed this oscillation between the two dimensions of Jerusalem, according to different emphasis: celestial or terrestrial, eternal or temporal, transcendent or immanent. For Christianity, beginning with Christ himself and the early Christian community, Jerusalem is no longer the center of a nation in this world, a terrestrial homeland, because the church is universal, extended to the whole "oikumene," including all nations, all races, all cultures, all civilizations. This means that Jerusalem is, above all, a spiritual reality. Thus, in the book of Revelation, Jerusalem appears as a bride coming down from heaven, as a city in the heavens (Rev 21). And in the first epistle of Peter, the church is a temple, a spiritual construction of which Christians are the living stones. In such a perspective, Jerusalem is a new and heavenly city beyond space and time, the center and the symbol of the kingdom of God in eternity.

This new significance of Jerusalem for Christianity is so evident and so fundamental that, during the middle ages, even at the time of the crusades, the terrestrial pilgrimage to the holy land was considered vain and useless. According to this medieval conception, the true home of a Christian is the celestial Jerusalem. Such was already the thought of many church fathers, like Gregory of Nyssa, Jerome, and Augustine. The kingdom of God is inside your heart, and the only true pilgrimage should be an interior one; the only urgent itinerary is the road to holiness, whose goal is the meeting with God in the Jerusalem of the heart.

We find a typical and beautiful manifestation of this spiritual meaning of Jerusalem in the Christian liturgy for the dedication of churches. As a temple in which dwells the divine presence, every church is a symbol, more precisely a sacrament, of the celestial Jerusalem, and also a symbol of the temple which is in every baptized person. This liturgy includes all the terminology of the Bible which relates to the dedication of the temple or the sanctity of Jerusalem—"*urbs Sion unica*" (unique city of Zion) and "*mansio mystica*" (mystical home), "*condita caelo*" (built in the Heaven) and prayers, antiphons and hymns filled with references to the book of Revelation.

This poetic symbolism is magnificent: the city of Jerusalem is indeed the model of every church, but it refers, in the final analysis, to the celestial Zion. One must beware of suppressing the realistic existence of the symbol in order to preserve the transcendence of the meaning. This was too often the tendency of the fathers of the church: a tendency to a kind of Platonism, a platonizing way of considering the signified reality without paying enough attention to the consistency of the symbol.

The mistake would be to stress so much the purely spiritual meaning of Jerusalem that one would come to forget that this city is also a city of this world, with a worldly and terrestrial life, a day-to-day history, flesh-and-blood citizens. Here we touch the very root of the attitude of some Christians who, in the present-day situation, fail to attach any terrestrial or existential value to the fact that Jewish identity and Jewish destiny are connected with the historical Jerusalem. In such an approach, Jerusalem retains its beautiful spiritual significance but, as a sacrament without matter, a eucharist without bread and wine, a poem without reference.

A balanced conception of the relationship between place and history, between past and memory, could overcome such a danger. It could be said, on this point, that Christian pilgrims rediscover the role of spiritual memory in the approach to the holy places. To visit a site or a landscape of the Hebrew Bible or the gospel is an occasion for remembering, just like the custom of the Jewish people during the celebration of Passover: "*Be'khol dor va'dor . . .*" "In every generation one is obliged to regard himself as though he himself had actually gone out of Egypt . . ." The recollection of the very night of the exodus is a way of being present at its permanent actuality. In the same manner, a pilgrimage to the holy places of the Bible is an occasion to recollect, to remind, to re-present, to make present, through the memory of faith, the actuality of the deeds and events which took place there.

We could express this "sacramental" attitude by quoting a verse from the book of Genesis: "*Vayifga bamaqom*" (28:11). "And [Jacob] touched the place." You know whom Jacob encountered during this night and what is the significance of "*Maqom*" in Jewish tradition. Jacob got in touch with God; he touched God through the place, whereupon stood the ladder connecting earth and heaven. Such an expression aptly describes the pilgrimage to Jerusalem: an experience in which the pilgrim, on this spot, in the earthly framework of this city, remembers the reality of the presence of God for our faith.

IV
AT THE CENTER OF THE ENCOUNTER

The return to Zion is a sign and condition of the return to God, meeting the mystery of salvation as it is externally present through the sacrament of Jerusalem. At the end of these reflections, I am struck by the fact that, for both of us, Jews and Christians, the fact of living in Jerusalem or in the holy land means a lasting invitation to remembrance and to hope, a continual demand of "self-transcendence." To live in Israel and especially in Jerusalem requires a particular stance toward Jewish identity as well as toward the calling to become a Christian: the demand to rediscover the eternal in the midst of time, unity despite differences and contradictions, peace in the midst of hostility and tension. Even more, for Jews and Christians, the message of Jerusalem seems like a proposal on God's part to read the events of time and history in the light of eternity, to respect differences and contradictions in full awareness of a shared aspiration to unity, and to build peace step by step on the strength of the desire and nostalgia which he has left in the human heart.

Passover, Pesach, passage: passage of man to God, of earth to heaven, of time to eternity. For Jews and for Christians Jerusalem is the city of passage, a city where exile and homeland are intertwined. In spite of and beyond their difficulties, Jews and Christians meet in the same posture before God. The paradox of break and continuity which both unites and separates them emerges here in a more striking way than anywhere else. So it is that Jerusalem, for a Christian, becomes that privileged place where he can discover Jewish identity in the same moment in which he becomes conscious of himself, recognizing what he has received from Israel.

So it is hardly surprising that Jerusalem becomes the meeting place par excellence. It is not the only such place, to be sure, yet the conditions here for encounter, for mutual recognition and dialogue, are at once more obvious and more imperative. Following the pattern of everything which touches Israel, whatever rapport one can realize here between Jews and Christians gains a worth at once unique and exemplary, singular and universal.

If I were to call to mind the progress accomplished over the last forty-five years—since the tragedy of the death camps, the return of the Jewish people to the land, and, more recently, the Vatican Council—I would recount it by discerning three stages in a progressive interiorization of mutual understanding.

First of all, it is clear that we have attained, as Jews and Christians, a stage in the dialogue where we can state to one another, without animosity certainly, yet also without fear or illusion, that we agree to disagree. We realize that Jesus separates us, that he is a sign of division and a stumbling block between us. But the very fact that we acknowledge one another and that we can speak so clearly with one another is itself a new reality.

Secondly, we are now able to acknowledge, from Jewish and Christian sides alike, without evasion or reticence, the Jewish identity of Jesus —his Jewishness. That is a new reality as well. We are no longer ashamed or afraid of this fact, which on one side or the other we used to find irritating or irrelevant. Yet Christian exegetes and theologians no longer hesitate to place Christ in the environment and tradition in which he came forth in the flesh, in their attempt to grasp the humanity of Jesus as a way of comprehending the reality of the incarnation. It is enough to cite the title of a recent book to express this new approach in a nutshell: *The Word Made Jew.* And we can see, on the Jewish side, a parallel progression in the direction of objectivity. Without acknowledging Jesus as Lord or messiah, to be sure, one no longer hesitates to acknowledge him as an offspring of the Jewish people. So it is that, in speaking to us of Jesus, one of the professors of New Testament at the Hebrew University in Jerusalem often said to us quite simply: "Adoni sheli, Adonai shelka (My master and your God [Lord])."

And there is even more. In the deeper and more intimate register of oratory and study, at that level of silence where Jews and Christians overhear one another in prayer and meet with a view to mutual discovery, objective yet faithful, we are beginning to discover, on the part of each, that Jesus the son of Israel reunites us in the very moment in which he divides us. This gives our encounter an utterly unique value, for we are in effect the only ones who experience this wrenching. Countless human beings of good will—animists, fetishists, Hindus, Shintos, even Muslims —have no reason at all to be upset by Jesus Christ, for they do not encounter him in their history nor does Jesus make reference to their tradition. Yet for a Jew, early or late, and especially in our time, his very person will elicit a question or even serve as a stumbling block. For our part, when we as Christians regard the break between Israel and the church, we cannot fail to suffer what François Lovsky has so accurately named "the wrenching absence." Yet this very wrenching marks us; we are the only ones so wounded. Paradoxically enough, it unites us—Jews and Christians—before the world, for it amounts to a family quarrel, a conflicted heritage. Yet this heritage is unique, for it has to do with a word addressed to humankind about its salvation, and we must bear witness to it together.

In this spirit, Israel and Jerusalem will be, without any doubt, the place where Jews and Christians can meet one another, according to the prayer with which, some years ago, a document of the French bishops concluded: "In a single movement of hope which will be a promise for the whole world."

Christian Attitudes Toward Israel and Jerusalem

Simon Schoon

A. CHRISTIAN PRESENCE

In the course of history, many forms have been sought and found to express the Christian attachment to the land of Israel and to Jerusalem. For some Christians this attachment led to the decision to settle in the land or in Jerusalem. A wide variety of Christian presence in Israel in our time witnesses to this attachment. The motivations for these various forms of Christian presence are very different and reflect many trends within Christianity that cannot be reduced to a common denominator.

The various Israel-theologies playing a role within the churches all over the world come to life, so to speak, in the concrete forms of Christian presence in the state of Israel. Precisely in the state of Israel or, as some prefer to say, in the holy land, Christians want their theological positions to be represented. This does not apply to all groups, in particular not to the largest group, that of the Arab Christians who do not need theological motivations for their presence in Israel as they have lived in the land for many centuries. Yet their presence also requires them, at times in spite of themselves, to reflect theologically on the phenomenon of the Jewish people and the state of Israel.

The various churches and groups in Israel, with their manifold motivations to be there, have very different interpretations of the notion and phenomenon of Israel. For some, Israel stands as proof that the end of time has arrived and that Jesus will return soon. Others see Israel as an oppressive power, confirming old anti-Jewish and antisemitic prejudices. For some, Israel is the sign of the return of the people of the Bible to the

Torah and the prophets. For others, Israel is the prototype of a modern, secularized state which should be called upon to convert.

Almost every church or group has developed its own Israel-theology. Usually a certain interaction can be seen between a particular presence and a theological view of Israel. Some forms of presence are even the direct product of a specific Israel-theology. The situation within the land adds new dimensions to these theological views. Yet, the same situation in the land of Israel is experienced quite differently by the various groups and is obviously not uniform.

Since all churches and Christian groups within Israel maintain links with church organizations and individuals in other countries, there is also interaction between those within Israel and those abroad regarding views of Israel.

The information passed by these mostly very well-functioning channels of communication can exercise a decisive influence on the opinions prevailing in Europe and America concerning various issues, such as freedom of religion in Israel, Jewish and Israeli identities, the Palestinian question, and the status of Jerusalem.[1]

It is difficult to give reliable statistics about the numbers of Christians in Israel, but a few words on this matter are necessary in order to provide some insight into the situation today. The Arab churches together form by far the largest group of Christians in Israel. At the same time they are a minority within a minority. The Arab sector constitutes about seventeen percent of Israeli citizenship. Within this minority, Arab Christians form a minority of about twenty percent within the Muslim majority. This means that Arab Christians constitute only two and one half percent of the Israeli population. Most other Christian groups, though, do not even account for one percentage point. The following survey renders an estimation, as official figures are lacking:

Greek Catholics (united with Rome)	30,000
Greek Orthodox	25,000
Roman Catholics	19,000
Maronites (united with Rome)	5,000
Armenians	2,500
Anglicans	1,700
Other Protestants	1,700
Copts	1,000

There are about 1,500 Jewish-Christians in Israel. Altogether, about twenty thousand Christians live in the area of Jerusalem, including eight hundred clergy serving about two hundred churches. Any classification of the churches and Christian groups in Israel must be somewhat arbitrary. The classification proposed here is, because of our specific subject, based upon the various groups' attitudes towards the Jewish state and their motivations, if existing, for living in Israel. Naturally, many motivating factors overlap from group to group and therefore several forms of Christian presence are not strictly separable. Within the various motivations, the whole gamut of Israel-theologies is reflected, as they play their roles elsewhere also. Below follows a classification which includes short characterizations of each form of presence.

I
ARAB CHRISTIANS:
CONFRONTATION IN SPITE OF THEMSELVES

Arab Christians in Israel live in confrontation with this state in spite of themselves. When in 1948 the Jewish state was founded, many cherished the hope that it would not be granted a long life and that it would quickly succumb to the dashing Arab armies. History, however, took a different course. The Arabs in Israel had to find a way to live with the reality of this history. From a majority they became in a short time a minority and experienced being strangers in their own land. Arab Christians often feel torn in their identity. In fact, they have to cope with three identities which are in collision with each other: they are Arabs, Christians, and Israelis.[2]

Their way of existing as churches and of living as Christians bears the stamp of their centuries-old position in the midst of dominating Islam. Explosions in the form of persecutions from Muslims occurred occasionally, but they were exceptions. They were second class citizens, however, in the Muslim states. Since most Arabs considered being an Arab synonymous to being a Muslim, many Christians felt the need to prove that they also could be good Arabs. To that end, many Arab Christians took the lead and found important positions in the Arab national movement and in the struggle against Zionism.[3]

In rejecting the Jewish state, Arab Christians are sometimes even more radical than Muslims. Numerous theological concepts of western origin have contributed to this. The doctrine of substitution, according to which the church has taken the place of Israel after Christ, has always been a prevalent view in the Eastern Orthodox churches. After 1967, when

Israel occupied the West Bank, the tensions within Israel have increased considerably, and since then a strong "Palestinization" has gotten under way.

Among Palestinian Arabs in Israel, in particular among Christians, a new intellectual elite has arisen since 1948 which takes more radical positions against Zionism than before. Arab theologians strictly distinguish between Judaism as a religion on the one hand and Zionism and the state of Israel on the other. This does not do justice to Jewish self-understanding,[4] but a balanced theological view can hardly be expected from people whose identity has been torn by the events of the last forty years.

Maybe a breakthrough in the entrenched positions of both sides could be expected from a dialogue between Jews and Arab Christians, two groups who as minorities have histories of suffering in the world at large and should be able, therefore, to find a common language. Yet up to now, dialogue has hardly begun. On both sides there are only individuals and small groups that deliberately opt for the painful path of dialogue and reconciliation. These courageous efforts are the only source of hope for the future.

II
JEWISH-CHRISTIANS:
AT HOME YET DOUBLY ALIENATED

It is helpful to make a distinction between those who find a home within the churches and those who organize themselves within more or less specifically Jewish-Christian groups. The latter prefer to call themselves "Messianic Jews," so as not to identify simply with "Gentile Christians." The former are automatically called "Notzrim" in Hebrew. To speak of a Jewish Christian sounds as strange to Jewish and Israeli ears as to speak of a Jewish Buddhist or a Jewish Hindu. Judaism strongly emphasizes the unity of the Jewish people and is strongly opposed to missionary attempts of other religions. With the smarting memories of the antisemitic history of the church, from the stakes in the middle ages up to the silence and complicity of the church during the Holocaust, Jews can only see the missionary tendency of the church toward Judaism as a spiritual "final solution" which ultimately aims at the same goal as Hitler's, the abolition of Judaism and the disappearance of the Jewish people. Opposition to mission, therefore, is in the eyes of Jews equal to faithfulness to their divine call as a people to be God's witnesses in history.

Against this background alone can one understand the strong anti-missionary attitude in Israeli society. The memory of the situation in the diaspora is still fresh in the minds of Israelis. For centuries, baptism was the entrance ticket to complete emancipation, to complete admission into society and culture. One could simply not believe that a Jew would ever convert to Christianity out of conviction, for that meant passing from the camp of the persecuted to that of the persecutors.

Some juridical pronouncements in this area reflect the predominant feelings in Israel. In 1962 the Jewish-Catholic priest Daniel Rufeisen, originally from Poland where he participated in the Jewish resistance movement during the Second World War, tried to get recognition as a Jew to whom the Law of Return would be applicable. Under this law, any Jew receives citizenship in the state of Israel immediately upon arrival in Israel if he or she so requests.

The lawsuit of Rufeisen before the High Court of Justice became one of the most remarkable proceedings in Israel's history. The judges rejected Rufeisen's request with a reference to the majority opinion of the Jewish people. A Jew who converts to another religion can no longer be considered a Jew and therefore does not come under the Law of Return.[5]

In 1979 a similar request was filed with the High Court by Eileen Dorflinger, and the same judgment was given. In fact, this time it was even sharper, as the combination of Jewishness and faith in Jesus as the messiah was deemed impossible. Thus we must conclude that the vast majority of the Jewish people do not agree with those who, either out of national feelings or religious conviction, want to continue to be considered Jews after they have passed over to the church or come to faith in Jesus. This involves for many Jewish-Christians in Israel and elsewhere major identity problems. They try to solve these problems in various ways. Some assimilate entirely into the existing churches; others, on the contrary, stress their Jewish identity as much as possible, observing shabbat and celebrating Jewish feasts; still others slowly disappear within the majority culture in Israel or return consciously to the synagogue.[6]

Many Jewish-Christians find themselves between a rock and a hard place. Within the church they feel misunderstood as Jews and they are often offended by latent anti-Jewish and sometimes even antisemitic expressions. Until recently they were also expected by the church to abandon their Jewishness completely upon their passage into Christianity. While they do not really feel at home in the church, at the same time they are rejected by their own people.

In Israel, on the one hand, they feel at home in the land of their ancestors; on the other hand, they continue to feel displaced because of rejection by their co-citizens.[7] In the diaspora they are often dismissed by non-Jews *together with* the Jewish people, but at the same time they are rejected *by* the Jewish people. Thus the Jewish-Christians find themselves in an unenviable position. Yet they often speak of themselves as "completed" Jews. They do not see themselves as having turned their back on their people, but they feel that their faith in Jesus has completed their Jewishness. Other Jews, however, will only see this conviction as an affirmation of the superiority feelings and triumphalistic attitude of Christianity.

Jewish-Christians often look for their "roots" in the first centuries of Christianity when a Church of the Circumcision existed next to the Gentile Christian church.[8] They continue to be challenged to find an expression of their own for their identity in these modern times, inspired by the model of the first Christian centuries. This, however, is far from simple because during the initial period of the church it was still accepted to combine being Jewish while believing in Jesus as messiah; but subsequently the roads of Judaism and Christianity have grown apart decisively. Jewish-Christians seem to have a difficult but important task in regard to the churches. They stand for the church as a reminder of the Jewish origins of Christianity and the Jewishness of Jesus, while also painfully embodying in themselves the depth of the rift between Christianity and Judaism. Thus they constitute a warning against facile and overly energetic attempts at harmonization.

III
MISSIONARY GROUPS:
THE FIELDS ARE RIPE FOR THE HARVEST

Although in Israel some missionaries are active among the Arab population, which in practice means mainly making proselytes among the native Orthodox churches, most missionary efforts are directed toward the Jewish majority in the state of Israel. An estimated several hundred people from abroad are active in Israel with undeniable missionary intentions. It is difficult to discern, though, the actual extent of the mission work because many activities are pursued in a quiet manner due to the violently anti-missionary attitude of the Israeli population.

Various Protestant churches, like the Scottish-Presbyterian Church and the Anglican Church, prefer an unobtrusive presence in which the Christian witness is perceptible mainly through all kinds of services.

These churches are linked together in the United Christian Council in Israel (U.C.C.I.). However, there also are numerous sectarian groups active in Israel that circulate tracts and New Testaments and that particularly attract the irritation of the Israeli population and of some Jewish organizations engaged in a struggle against missionary organizations.[9]

There is a growing tendency, especially in the U.C.C.I., which stresses the need to contextualize the missions of the churches and thereby draws attention to the specific situation in Israel and to the necessity of the churches to become indigenous.[10] The criticism, however, which these churches and groups incur is that they are not alive enough to the particular character of the Jewish people by putting them on one line with all other nations and classifying them under the general denominator of the "great commission" (Mt 18:18–20). The secularization in Israel is generally seen as an unique occasion for the missions to proclaim the message of the gospel in a certain vacuum. The tendency remains to depict Judaism in somber colors in order to stimulate the motivation to missionize. Usually the breach between Judaism and Christianity is accentuated as sharply as possible, and attempts at dialogue are ordinarily seen as a compromising and watering down of standpoints.

IV

MILLENARIAN GROUPS: IT WILL HAPPEN HERE SOON

The borderlines between millenarian and missionary groups are dim, but the more outspoken millenarian groups are usually anti-missionary. Their motivation to be present in Israel is connected with the belief that the return of the Jews to the land greatly accelerates the approach of the end of times and that the Jews will soon convert to the messiah *en masse*. They are convinced that God himself will in his time open the eyes of the Jews for the glory of Jesus Christ. In the meantime, their task is best described by the Pauline term of "making the Jews jealous" (Rom 11:14). They also sometimes speak of the "service of comforting," in reference to Isaiah 40:1: "Comfort, comfort my people." Usually, Old Testament prophecies are explained literally, in a fundamentalistic way, and are brought into direct connection with current events.[11]

Millenarians adhere to various doctrines and explain Bible passages in various ways. Some groups identify with the ten lost tribes. Especially in the United States, the doctrine of dispensationalism has found many adherents, by whom history is divided into several dispensations, including one for Israel and one for the Christian Church. These latter groups send many representatives to Israel.

When the state of Israel is seen simply as a fulfillment of Old Testament prophecies, an absolute support of the politics of each government of this state is the consequence. Often these Christians have almost nothing to do with politics elsewhere in the world, leaving that gladly to the politicians. Yet for Israel they make an exception, as this is for them a matter of faith. One can hardly blame Israel for accepting the support of these groups with sympathy. Yet one can also hear critical voices in Israel that warn against a "conditional love" on the part of these Christians who show little openness to or appreciation for the religious aspects of Judaism. They interpret the political situation of today simply as the setting of the stage for the imminent events of the end time.

V
GUARDIANS OF THE HOLY PLACES:
ON THE SPOT WHERE IT ALL BEGAN

Many Christians refer to Israel primarily as the "holy land." They are particularly devoted to a number of holy places in this country. Most of the holy sites are in the possession of the Greek Orthodox, Roman Catholics, and Armenians. The partition of the Church of the Holy Sepulchre, called the Church of the Resurrection by the Orthodox, among the "big three" and a number of smaller churches, is very complicated and has been the source of endless quarrels and skirmishes through the ages.[12]

Protestants are not very impressed by these places and prefer to be inspired by the sight of the Sea of Galilee or the view of Jerusalem from the Mount of Olives. But they also control the "garden tomb" in Jerusalem which is an "alternative" tomb of Jesus, visited by many devout Protestant pilgrims. The Roman Catholic Franciscans have controlled several of the most important holy places since the crusades through their *custodia*. The Greek Orthodox and Armenians, however, trace their claims back to the first centuries.

They are all interested in preserving the status quo, as the situation is called by a characteristic technical term. As long as the status quo was kept by the civil authorities, the guardians of the holy places maintained good relations with each government that has been in power in the holy land and the holy city over the centuries.

On June 22, 1967, after the Six Day War, the Knesset passed the "Protection of Holy Places Law," in which Israel guarantees free access to all faithful to all holy places. In Israel the traumatic memory of the period between 1948 and 1967 is still alive, when Christians were allowed to visit Jordan-controlled Jerusalem and Bethlehem but Jews were forbidden to pray at the Western Wall.

The presence of the guardians of the holy places reminds us, on one hand, of the abominable "God wants it" ideology of the crusaders, but on the other hand they have preserved something of the original Christian attachment to Jerusalem and of the concrete, this-worldly character of biblical revelation. The rejection of this attachment to holy spots in the Protestant tradition is often connected with a spiritualization of the revelation. The holy places can serve as a reminder of the concreteness of God's revelation in the past and, at the same time, of the concreteness of God's promises for the future. But attachment to isolated holy places can narrow our faith perspective if it obscures the significance of the land as a whole, or blinds us to the living witness of the people now residing there.

VI
RELIGIOUS ORDERS: HEEDING THE CALL

There are scores of religious orders and thousands of religious devotees present in Israel. Some live a strictly contemplative life and hardly come into contact with the outside world. Others have dedicated themselves to study or to spiritual service. The community of Lavra Netofa in the Galilee, under the direction of the former Dutch priest Jacob Willebrands, deserves to be mentioned for its endeavors to infuse new life into the Palestinian monastic ideal and to work for reconciliation between Jews and Arabs.

The Order of the Little Sisters and Brothers of Jesus also comes to the fore as a group integrating as far as possible into the normal life in Israel, in the Jewish as well as the Arab milieu. This order does not missionize but seeks, through a hidden life of prayer, to put the presence of Christ into the midst of society. The order's brothers and sisters all have full-time jobs and live among the people. Their life is in response to a call, a call to share everything with their fellow men.

VII
SOLIDARITY GROUPS:
FROM A BASIS OF HISTORICAL RESPONSIBILITY

The Christian settlement of Nes Ammim in the Galilee is an example of a group based on the idea of solidarity with Israel.[13] This writer participated in the project for six and a half years and lived there with his family.

Due to the initiative of some Dutch and Swiss people, Nes Ammim was established in the 1960s as a cooperative community (*moshav*).

In December 1960, Levi Eshkol, minister of finance and later prime minister of Israel, was offered a memorandum outlining the project. In 1962, two hundred and seventy-five acres of land were purchased from a Druze sheikh, spurring a controversy within Israel. Prime Minister Eshkol was violently attacked by the religious parties within his coalition, as they feared missionary activities were Nes Ammim's intention. As a result of the publicity storm which ensued, plans for the establishment of the village were frozen. The Israeli government gave its formal assent to the establishment of the village in January 1964, and by the end of that year some twenty-five people had begun the pioneering work at Nes Ammim, the name of which was taken from Isaiah 11:10, "sign of the nations."

Nes Ammim was designed as an international and inter-church project. There have been many discussions and problems regarding the aim of Nes Ammim, but from the beginning it was made clear to Israel and to the churches that mission among the Jews was not intended. Two pioneers, Johan Pilon and Shlomo Bezek, a Christian and a Jew, led Nes Ammim through the turbulent pioneer years. Many within the churches could not follow the new road in Jewish-Christian relations opened by these two men, and this caused many conflicts in the early years.

The integration of the community into the Jewish society, as for example in celebrating the shabbat meal on Friday evening with the whole community and holding the church service on shabbat morning, caused some controversy. A village and encounter center was opened in 1975 and a guest house in 1981. Encounter and discussion take an increasingly important place as the pioneer years draw to a close. There were approximately one hundred and eighty-five inhabitants in 1983. The village is supported by organizations in four countries and receives about 24,000 visitors annually. The Israelis consider Nes Ammim an integral part of the multi-colored landscape of Israel. Nes Ammim may be described as a project of Christian presence, a sign of solidarity, or a project of service.

Solidarity with Israel is not the exclusive characteristic of groups like Nes Ammim, but in describing the motivating force for this form of presence that key word keeps turning up. Solidarity is based on the conviction that there is a special relationship of the Christian church toward the Jewish people, and on the awareness that the church bears historical responsibility with regard to Israel because of centuries of anti-Judaic and antisemitic undertones of church history. Solidarity with the Jewish people brought Nes Ammim to the principle of a strictly non-missionary presence in Israel. Nes Ammim seeks to contribute to the Israeli economy and, overall, to show solidarity by preparedness to share the life in Israel, with all its problems and dangers. Besides work, study is highly valued. Each year hundreds of people go to Nes Ammim to participate in some form of study program. The Jewish roots of Christianity and various themes of Jewish-Christian dialogue are especially emphasized.

Nes Ammim has been accepted in the Galilee, after some initial resistance. The Christian presence of Nes Ammim is considered by Israelis, Jews and Arabs, as an opportunity for exchange of thought, discussion, and encounter.

VIII
ORGANIZATIONS FOR STUDY AND DIALOGUE:
ON THE ROAD TOGETHER

While very few of the groups mentioned consider study and dialogue unimportant, certain organizations and institutions in Israel concentrate specifically and exclusively on it. Examples are the Ecumenical Institute for Theological Research-Tantur, the Ecumenical Theological Research Fraternity, and the Swedish Theological Institute.

It is pointed out that there are Hieronymus types and Helena types among the Christians in Israel.[14] Empress Helena looked for the origins of Christianity by searching for holy places and building basilicas upon them. Church father Hieronymus looked for the roots of his faith by studying Hebrew and the scriptures, which came into being in the holy land. Nowadays, the Helena types are guarding the holy places. The Hieronymus types are attracted to Israel because its soil is full of archeological treasures and its libraries are full of books and manuscripts. Hieronymus types, however, sometimes run the risk of forgetting that human beings are still living and breathing in Israel and that the deep wounds of many past conflicts are not yet healed by far.

B. CHRISTIAN ATTITUDES

To exemplify the attitudes of the various forms of Christian presence toward Israel, we can best look at the various Christian views of Jerusalem. It is not easy to pinpoint what attaches Christians to Jerusalem. The mainstreams of Christianity—Roman Catholic, Eastern Orthodox, Protestant—hold different opinions. For Eastern Christians, Jerusalem is an important center of pilgrimage. The west also has this tradition, as was shown by the crusades which, among other things, aimed at safeguarding pilgrimages to Jerusalem.

Many Protestants, however, hold the opinion that Jerusalem has no significance whatsoever after Christ. After the crucifixion and resurrection, the role of the earthly Jerusalem came to an end. Christians are now pilgrims toward a heavenly Jerusalem. The persistence of the Jews in valuing earthly Jerusalem is seen as obstinacy and blindness.

In speaking about Jerusalem, the New Testament seems to contain a tension between rupture and continuity with Jewish tradition. The apostle Paul reveals on the one hand a deep rift with his past, in speaking about "the present Jerusalem, in slavery with her children" (Gal 4:25). On the other hand, there is continuity in his life when he goes up to Jerusalem in imitation of Jesus (Acts 21:12–13). Paul kept returning to this city, and he saw Jerusalem as the center from which he undertook his missionary travels. His elaborate efforts among the Gentile Christian communities to collect aid for the mother community in Jerusalem, which he calls his "service for Jerusalem" (Rom 15:31), illustrate his attachment to the city.[15]

The destruction of the Temple in 70 C.E. was interpreted by Christians as God's judgment on the sinful Jerusalem. After the year 70, the Jewish mother community in Jerusalem lost its authority. In the letter to the Hebrews, one can see that cult, temple, sacrifice, and priesthood had developed a totally different meaning for the Jewish Christians. Christ is the only high priest and his sacrifice is effective once and for all. Christians are exhorted to share the shame of Christ by going "outside the camp," for "we have no lasting city, but we seek the city which is to come" (Heb 13:11–14).

Should Christians today only go along with this late development in the New Testament? Do Jesus' burning love of Jerusalem and Paul's orientation toward it have nothing to say to us anymore? Can we still speak of a Christian attachment to Jerusalem? We shall look, somewhat schematically, into the various Christian attitudes concerning Jerusalem. For Jews, Jerusalem is the focal point of the unity between land and people. Also in Christian reflections about the land of Israel, Jerusalem functions more or less as a concentration point. We can distinguish the following models of approach.

I
SPIRITUALIZATION OF JERUSALEM

Paul's sharp words about law and grace in his letter to the Galatians seem to be directed in particular against "Judaizing" Gentile Christians and not against Jews or Jewish Christians, and his midrash in Galatians 4:21–31 in which Jerusalem is called a city in slavery of the law can only be explained within his traditional rabbinical approach toward scripture. Nonetheless, these Bible passages have had a considerable influence on Christian thinking about Jerusalem. "The city built so high," as a Christian hymn says, has become exclusively the heavens, a Jerusalem to which Christians, "beyond earth and stars," hope to ascend after death, "free from the earthly, satiated with this-worldly joys." Within this climate of thinking, discontinuity with Jewish tradition is stressed. The destruction of Jerusalem in 70 C.E. is seen as the final end of the Jewish Jerusalem with its temple and sacrificial service. The Jerusalem of today has no significance whatsoever for these Christians, except perhaps to illustrate to them the Jewish "stubbornness" in pursuing an earthly instead of a heavenly Jerusalem.

II
IDEALIZATION OF JERUSALEM

Many Christians have great difficulties locating the city of Jerusalem as a concrete site on the map. They also idealize the Jews as a people without a land, imposing on Israel an exile ideal. Jerusalem then becomes an idea which symbolizes the assignment of all people to work for justice and reconciliation in the world. It cannot be identified any longer with a specific site; it is both everywhere and nowhere. Jerusalem is wherever justice is being done. Those who try to materialize shalom on this earth are in reality the legal inhabitants of "Jerusalem." Yet, should not the imitation of Christ mean that Christians, like Jesus, continue to adhere to the tangibility of the earthly Jerusalem? If Jerusalem can be located everywhere and nowhere, is there a danger that, ultimately, Zion also is nowhere to be found, just an inaccessible utopia?

III
JERUSALEM AS SACRAMENT

Eastern Orthodox and Roman Catholic Christians have more feelings than Protestants for the specific holiness of Jerusalem. As places of God's special revelation, the land and Jerusalem in particular are for them points of concentration of a certain message. Pilgrimages to the holy land and especially to Jerusalem connect the participants in a special way with the divine revelation those places proclaim. At the most holy places, the liturgy should be celebrated and prayers said. Jerusalem is a sacramental reality par excellence because in this city the holy sepulchre preserves the memory of the concreteness and physicality of Christ's resurrection. The city is also a sacrament, a sign pointing to the matter signified, to the reality of the resurrection.

The holy places are the means to come into contact with the mystery of Christ, which one is able to receive only through faith.[16] This outlook, however, generally allows for little understanding of the Jewish attachment to Jerusalem, as it lacks the view of Judaism as a living reality. Most of the time, the church is considered the "new Israel."

IV
JERUSALEM AS THE CITY OF THE END-TIME

Some Christians see certain prophecies concerning the end of times as being fulfilled in our lifetime in Israel and in Jerusalem. They particularly look at the unification of Jerusalem in 1967 as the beginning of that end time. They point to the fact that the whole world and the United Nations are continuously concerned about Jerusalem. In this framework they mention Zechariah 12:2–3: "Lo, I am about to make Jerusalem a cup of reeling to all the peoples round about. . . . On that day will I make Jerusalem a heavy stone for all the peoples; all who lift it shall grievously hurt themselves. And all the nations of the earth will come together against it." Luke 21:24 is another cherished text, in which they see the end of Jerusalem's oppression and the unification of 1967 foretold, as Jesus says in his apocalyptical discourse: "Jerusalem will be trodden down by the Gentiles, until the times of the Gentiles are fulfilled" (cf. Mt 23:37; Lk 13:34). However, it is an irresponsible way of Bible study to isolate texts from their context and to apply them directly to the situation of today.

V
JERUSALEM AS A SIGN OF THE CONCRETENESS
OF GOD'S PROMISE

Jerusalem certainly points to a spiritual reality and to an ethical ideal in many ways, but it should not be spiritualized or degraded to an idea. Also for Christians, Jerusalem is primarily the sign of the return of the Jews to the land. Their concrete return into history, after the hell of Auschwitz, is most movingly illustrated by the image of children playing in the streets of Jerusalem. Christians should respect the Jewish identity, in which Jerusalem takes such a central place.[17]

Jerusalem for Christians is also a sign of the concreteness of God's promises. The holy places connect us not only with the past but even more with the future. Christians are reminded of the concreteness and earthliness of the redemption which has become and will become visible in our world.

Paul's expectation for the future was connected to his hope for Israel. One purpose of his missionary travels was "to make Israel jealous" (Rom 11:13–14). He worked for the "harvesting of the full number of the Gentiles" in order to realize the vision of the procession of the nations going up to Zion. All this would end by "all Israel being saved," when, in his expectation, "the deliverer will come from Zion" (Rom 11:26). Leaving out all kind of hermeneutical problems, we may state that we should learn from Paul, as twentieth century Christians, that our future expectation should never dissociate itself from Jerusalem and Zion.

Does not Jerusalem as a place for encounter between Jews, Christians, and Muslims also include a promise for the oecumene of all humanity which Psalm 87 envisions? Respect for dead sites in Jerusalem, holy places for Jews, Christians and Muslims, should never replace openness and attentiveness to living human beings. The concrete Jerusalem, in the midst of today's political confusion, reminds us of our concrete commission to fight for the humanity of mankind.[18] In this sense, Jerusalem reminds us of God's dream, the dream of shalom.

NOTES

1. See e.g. H. Fishman, *American Protestantism and a Jewish State* (Detroit: Wayne State Univ. Press, 1973), pp. 174–179.

2. Cf. S. Samooha, *Israel: Pluralism and Conflict* (London: Routledge & Kegan Paul, 1978), pp. 45–47, 102–103, 197–199; also K. Cragg, *This Year in Jerusalem: Israel in Experience* (London: Darton, Longmans and Todd, 1982), pp. 50–88.

3. Cf. R.B. Betts, *Christians in the Arab East: A Political Study* (Athens: Lycabetus Press, 1975), pp. 138–203.

4. Cf. P. Loeffler, *Arabische Christen im Nahostkonflikt: Christen im politischen Spannungsfeld* (Frankfurt: Otto Lembeck, 1976).

5. S.Z. Abramov, *Perpetual Dilemma: Jewish Religion in the Jewish State* (New Jersey: Assoc. University Presses, 1976), pp. 285–290; S.N. Herman, *Israelis and Jews: The Continuity of an Identity* (Philadelphia: Jewish Publication Society, 1970), pp. 91–95.

6. B.Z. Sobel, *Hebrew Christianity: The Thirteenth Tribe* (New York: John Wiley, 1974), pp. 175–320.

7. Cf. B. Bagatti, *The Church of the Circumcision* (Jerusalem: Franciscan Printing Press, 1971); F. Manns, *Essais sur le Judeo-Christianisme* (Jerusalem: Franciscan Printing Press, 1977).

8. O.C.M. Kvarme, "The Development of Hebrew Christianity: Credal and Ecclesiological Questions—The Problem of Contextualization," in D.-M. Jaeger, ed., *Christianity in the Holy Land* (Jerusalem: Tantur Ecumenical Institute, 1981), pp. 315–342.

9. Cf. a one-sided description of the situation in the 1960s: P. Osterbye, *The Church in Israel: A Report on the Work of the Christian Churches in Israel, with Special Reference to the Protestant Churches and Communities* (Lund: Gleerup Bokfoerlag, 1970).

10. O.C.M. Kvarme, ed., *Let Jews and Arabs Hear His Voice* (Jerusalem: The United Christian Council in Israel, 1981).

11. E.g. H. Lindsey, *The Late Great Planet Earth* (Michigan: Zondervan Publishing, 1972); E.A. Josephson, *Israel, God's Key to World Redemption* (Kansas: Bible Light Publications, 1974).

12. Cf. S.P. Colbi, *Christianity in the Holy Land: Past and Present* (Tel Aviv: Am Hassefer, 1969).

13. S. Schoon/H. Kremers, *Nes Ammim-Ein christliches Experiment in Israel* (Neukirchen-Vluyn: Neukirchener Verlag, 1978).

14. J. Schoneveld, "Dialogue with Jews," in *Immanuel* (1976) 6, pp. 61–69.

15. J. Munck, *Paulus und die Heilsgeschichte* (Aarhus, 1954), pp. 293–300; K.F. Nickle, "The Collection: A Study in Paul's Strategy," in *Studies on Biblical Theology* 48 (London, 1966).

16. L. Volken, "Sinn und Botschaft des Heiligen Landes," in D.-M. Jaeger, ed., *Christianity in the Holy Land* (Jerusalem: Tantur Ecumenical Institute, 1981), pp. 97–118.

17. Cf. D. Hartman, "Jerusalem: Confrontation and Challenge," in *Immanuel* (1975) 5, 94–101.

18. Cf. also I. Greenberg, "Cloud of Smoke, Pillar of Fire: Judaism, Christianity and Modernity after the Holocaust," in Eva Fleischner, ed., *Auschwitz; Beginning of a New Era?* (New York: KTAV/ADL, 1977), pp. 7–55.

Territory and Morality from a Religious Zionist Perspective

Uriel Simon

TRADITION AS FOUNDATION

The perspective I bring to this interreligious discussion is that of an Israeli Jew whose father is Abraham, whose master is Moses, whose poet-king is David, whose admonishers and consolers are Amos, Isaiah, and Jeremiah, whose sages are the wise Pharisees Rabbi Yohanan ben Zakkai and Rabbi Akiva, whose rabbis are Maimonides and Nachmanides, whose heroes are the pioneers who rebuilt and defended the state of Israel, and whose brothers and sisters are the six million slaughtered Jews. From all of them I have inherited a passionate loyalty to the Jewish people and to the holy land of Israel, together with a fundamental commitment to the Torah ideals of justice, peace, and the sanctity of human life. It is my strong conviction that these biblical ideals not only are the true source of religious Zionism, but are also its corrective principles.

For one thing, the Hebrew prophets themselves, those courageous champions of justice and righteousness, those visionaries who foresaw a messianic reign of peace—it was they who prophesied an "ingathering of the exiles," the homecoming of the people of Israel to the land of Israel. This entails our deliverance from diaspora, minority existence, through the restoration of Jewish national sovereignty centered in Jerusalem. Isaiah, for example, could reconcile his vision of national homecoming with universalist ideals: "Zion will be redeemed through justice, and those who return to her through righteousness" (Is 1:27).

NATIONALITY AND ETHICS

This vision of redemption, combining national particularism and universalist ethics, is the characteristic (if not unique) message which Judaism proclaims as a world religion embodied in the life of a particular people. On this basic point, Judaism differs from Christianity and Islam. These other two faith traditions are non-national, or trans-national, virtually denying national distinctiveness as a religious value. In principle, the church universal, or the Islamic *umma,* can be so extensive as to embrace all of humanity. And in practice, both traditions have exhibited proselytizing tendencies based on the wish to see this potential all-inclusiveness realized.

Judaism, on the whole, resisted the temptation to wage missionary crusades (even non-violent ones) because the Abrahamic covenant, renewed at Sinai with the entire people, calls us to become a "kingdom of priests and a holy people" (Ex 19:6). The charge to be a priestly people is not an invitation to establish a segregated enclave divorced from the needs and aspirations of all humanity. Rather, it is a challenge to assume special responsibilities toward all of humankind, indeed toward the whole creation, by creating an exemplary society that reflects Torah teachings and spreads life-enhancing blessings beyond itself.

In a paradoxical way, it is the particularistic character of Judaism that enables it to remain basically tolerant toward other monotheistic believers. According to Catholic doctrine—I do not know to what extent it still holds today—there is no salvation outside the walls of the church. And according to Islamic doctrine, the world is divided between *Dar al-Islam* and *Dar al-Harb,* the domain of Islam and the domain of war, and the latter is to be annexed to the former. The Jewish national religion demands of faithful, practicing Jews the fulfillment of 613 commandments and promises salvation to those non-Jews who fulfill the seven Noachide commandments. When I speak with young Israelis, I often write on the blackboard "7 vis-à-vis 613," and I say, "these excessive demands are the true meaning and the justification of our chosenness."

I understood for the first time what the strange metaphor "a kingdom of priests" means when I was a student and paid a visit to Britain. I went to an inexpensive youth hostel and was put in a room with a Catholic boy from Genoa. We discussed our respective religions in broken English late into the night. He told me that, in good Italian families, one son becomes a priest, the second one takes over the business, the third one becomes a doctor, etc. I asked him what it means to be a priest, and he said it meant celibacy and the renunciation of private property. I was stunned, for I saw the seriousness of such a burden. Then this fellow asked me what it meant to be a Jew. I said, "You know, in all of London I can eat in only two restaurants, and I pray three times a day, keep the sabbath, and so on."

Now *he* was stunned. Then I said, "We, all of us, are a people of priests. Less is demanded of us than of your priests. You cannot demand of a whole people that its members live in monasteries. We live in families, in businesses, in the wider society. But compared to other peoples, we are commanded to be priests."

To clarify what it means for the Jewish people to aspire to a "priestly" role and holiness in collective terms, two points are worth emphasizing. The first is that the people are not intrinsically or ontologically holy. At birth, Jews are no different from any other human beings. The distinctiveness of Jews lies in our special destiny, not in any special essence. Any favor we Jews may be worthy of in the eyes of God is totally conditioned on our behavior. To become a holy nation of priests, we have to live an intensive religious life that includes moral integrity as the conscious focus, not merely ritual purity. This is the central message of the Hebrew prophets, reiterated many times in our scriptures. The blessings promised to us are conditioned on our faithfulness to God and his Torah. Any other interpretation of chosenness can easily become a racist or chauvinist perversion of the true idea, and may lead to self-righteousness rather than self-criticism and humility.

The second point, which derives from this understanding of Jewish identity and responsibility, is that Jews are given extra obligations by our creator, not additional rights or privileges. Failure to appreciate this basic point may lead one to embrace the same kind of triumphalism that has colored much of Christian and Islamic thinking throughout the centuries —and we Jews have paid a very high price for that "religious" superiority on the part of others.

CHOSENNESS

Has the Jewish people in the course of its long history ever achieved holiness? How could it? If you read the Hebrew Bible, you will find on almost every page severe admonitions for not living up to the standard set before us at Sinai. We cannot and should not claim that we have fulfilled the demands in the Torah, but we always have its challenges to inspire us and guide our actions. The ideals of justice, righteousness, and peace are not only prophetic ideals; they are also practical imperatives that must be translated into everyday behavior wherever we happen to live as Jews.

And if we live in the land of Israel, as a reconstituted sovereign nation, then the burden takes on even graver dimensions. For the responsibilities that come with political and military power are the true litmus test of Torah ethics. Hebrew prophecy presupposes Jewish power, a Jewish sovereign commonwealth with a head of state and ruling establishment always under the judgment of the almighty sovereign of the universe. As a religious Jew and citizen of the state of Israel, I am constantly aware of the "mixed blessing" which statehood and power bestow upon me. But given the history of persecution we have endured when we lacked power, and given the socio-political framework which the Torah expects us to establish in the holy land, I would opt for the moral and spiritual dilemmas of empowerment over the dilemmas that come with powerlessness.

TWO PEOPLES

After centuries of vulnerability and persecution, culminating in genocide, and after a series of wars with our Arab neighbors in the Middle East, some religious Jews in Israel have concluded that the supreme test which God has set before us is whether we have the strength of faith to fight our enemies until we win the battle with God's help. This kind of reaction to our historical experience is understandable, but it is also regrettable and potentially dangerous. For it can produce a religious sensibility that may be termed "fear of heaven without a fear of sin." It makes of justice, righteousness, and even peace distorted parodies of these moral ideals, for they become warped by a self-referencing lens that defines goodness by whatever is good for us. And since we have suffered so much in the past, it is easy to succumb to this self-serving position without feeling too many qualms of conscience.

In Israel, where we face real enemies, who have declared their intention to destroy the Jewish state, the threat is grasped in terms of a second holocaust, which reinforces the tendency in certain circles to mystify the conflict, i.e. to turn it into a metaphysical confrontation between God and Satanic forces (Amalekites, for example). Such an attitude makes the notion of justice or peace based on political compromise totally outrageous, even sacrilegious.

Such circles, which unfortunately constitute a sizeable minority in Israel, cannot integrate the notion that the Palestinian people has legitimate claims, too, as a self-constituted nation dwelling in the same homeland. The refusal by the Palestinian leadership, until very recently, to honor the Jewish national aspiration to self-determination compounds this self-justifying stance on the part of too many Israelis. And, as a result, they are unable or unwilling to engage in the kind of prophetic self-criticism that is demanded of us.

As a human act within history, the establishment of the state of Israel naturally involved injustices, the commission of certain sins (principally the expulsion of Palestinian civilians). Especially since the state was born in a bloody war waged against it, and it has been fighting for its very existence ever since, the partisan perception of "us or them" has led—on both sides—to hostile and exclusive, rather than conciliatory and inclusive, policies. The question for all of us, Jews and Palestinians, is whether we stick to the self-destructive indulgence of ethical double standards, justifying all our actions and condemning the same deeds when committed by the other side, or whether both peoples can overcome this tragic dynamic and forge a just peace based on mutual respect and common interests.

Both Jews and Palestinians will have to settle for less than total sovereignty over the whole land, if they truly want the land to be sanctified by righteous living rather than desecrated by injustice and the shedding of blood. To express this ethical/political stand in traditional Jewish terms (especially as other religious Jews view territorial partition as unacceptable), we must examine what the holiness of the land really means, just as we considered what the holiness of the people Israel ought to mean.

HOLINESS OF THE LAND

Just as God created Adam (i.e. humankind) and chose Abraham (i.e. Israel) to be a blessing to all the nations, so he created heaven and earth and chose the land of Israel. From the perspective of creation, the children of Israel are totally equal to all other human beings (children of Adam and Noah). Therefore, the Jewish person or people is not endowed with any holy essence, but is called to aspire to holiness through fulfilling God's commandments. In a parallel fashion, the holy land is not bestowed with an intrinsic, ontological holiness beyond other parts of the creation. Its holiness, too, is functional: it was chosen to be the seat of the "kingdom of priests." In fact, the term "land of Israel" appears for the first time in the Bible only in 1 Samuel 13:19. Why is that? And why, until then, is it referred to as the "land of Canaan," which (for Jewish ears) is even more scandalous than the Roman name "Palestine," commemorating the Philistines.

I would submit that this negative fact implies that the land is imprinted by the deeds of its inhabitants, and it is thus left to us to transform the land of Canaan into the land of Israel. Since holiness does not reside in the physical landscape of the land chosen by the almighty to be the land of

Israel, there is no guarantee that, by returning to this landscape, we will be endowed with an extra measure of holiness ourselves. Rather, it is our task to sanctify the land through our level of religious and moral commitment to Torah. For the land was, and always is, only a medium, a vessel, just as the people Israel remains a medium or vessel for holiness. And the two vessels are organically connected. The land of Israel is the locus of Israel's religious and national self-realization. The land waits for us to come and live in it, according to the Torah teachings that instruct us on how to hallow the whole ecology of the land, how to relate to the soil which is the Lord's (cf. Lev 25:22), to the trees and animals, and most importantly to our fellow human beings (including the non-Jew in our midst). And if we fail to live up to these teachings, then the land can "vomit" us out again into exile, just as it had "vomited" out the Canaanites (cf. Lev 18:28). No one, including the Jews, has an unconditional right to dwell in the holy land; everyone dwells here, so to speak, "on probation."

LAND AND STATE OF ISRAEL

What is the most pertinent political implication of this religious teaching? It is that, for our state to be truly Jewish, it will have to be smaller in geographic area than the whole of the holy *land* of Israel. Otherwise the *state* of Israel inevitably represses the national will of the Palestinians and perpetuates a regime of institutionalized injustice, i.e. a separate set of laws and punishments for Palestinians, harsher than those applied to Jews. Such a regime is both unjust and un-Jewish, according to the fundamental biblical injunction: "One standard of justice shall you have, for the stranger and the citizen alike, for I the Lord am your God" (Lev 24:22).

Deplorably, not all religious Jews, in Israel or elsewhere, share this ethical and political outlook. The mistrust and resentment caused by our own past suffering is part of the reason for a more belligerent and less compassionate stance on the part of many Jews. Such feelings are natural and understandable, given our history. Less forgivable, in my view, is the ideological dimension which is quite often reinforced by these feelings. Israeli schoolchildren are being overzealously fed on Rashi's commentary to Genesis 1:1. Our greatest commentator on the Hebrew scriptures questions the inclusion of the historical book of Genesis within the Torah, which is essentially a practical guidebook for Jewish living. His answer: the creation story is the basis of our inheriting the land of Canaan. His prooftext: "He has shown his people the power of his works, that he may give them the heritage of the nations" (Ps 111:6)—meaning that the whole earth belongs to the creator, who thus has full authority to terminate the right of possession of the Canaanites and transfer it to Israel. When this interpretation is applied to the demands of our present situation, it is understood to mean that Israel's exclusive claim on the entire land is based on divine will, which cannot be measured by human ethical standards. In such a theological framework, any Palestinian national claims are rendered meaningless.

It should be pointed out that this midrash which Rashi records at the beginning of his Torah commentary is by no means either the exclusive or the necessary interpretation. Nor is it the most convincing argument for the inclusion of the creation story and the lives of the patriarchs in the Bible. It was, in fact, challenged by Ramban (Nachmanides) in his commentary on the same verse. He raises the following difficulty: It is not reasonable to suppose that the book of Genesis is intended merely to teach us that the world was created by God; for, if that were so, it would have sufficed to say "for in six days the Lord created the heavens and the earth . . ." as is mentioned in the ten commandments included in the book of Exodus (20:11). According to Nachmanides, the whole book of Genesis is intended to teach us that our hold on the land is *conditional* on our obedience to God's word. Following the act of creation, we are told of a whole series of expulsions that are punishments for sinning: Adam and Eve from the garden, Cain becoming a wanderer after murdering his brother Abel, and the children of Israel descending to Egypt because of the sins of their forefathers. This principle is clearly expressed in the warning issued to the people of Israel on the eve of their settling in the "promised land": they should beware of following in the ways of the Canaanites, lest the land reject them, too (Lev 18:28).

So we have an alternative understanding to the one so enthusiastically derived from Rashi's commentary. The master of the universe intended the land of Israel for the people of Israel, but only in conjunction with the severe admonition that our actual hold on the land is conditioned on our behavior. There is a need for this warning, for clinging to the dangerous illusion that God will be on our side, unconditionally, by virtue of our covenant with him, may lead us to sin. In light of this, it would be appropriate for Jewish educators to always couple the verse which Rashi cites (Ps 111:6)—"He has shown his people the power of his works, that he may give them the heritage of the nations"—with the verse immediately following: "The works of his hands are truth and justice; all his commandments are trustworthy." God's power is not exerted in an arbitrary or amoral manner, and he does not give his people the heritage of other nations except in accordance with truth and justice. It follows that we are commanded not only to believe in God's sovereignty over the whole creation, but also in his justice as the Father and judge of all humanity.

CONFLICT OF VALUES

Certainly, anyone like myself, who believes in the sanctity of *Eretz Yisrael* and in the divine promise of it to the people of Israel, finds himself in a state of inner conflict between this theological conviction and the moral conviction that the regaining of Israel's freedom should not be done at the price of suppressing the freedom of another people. A way to resolve this conflict of values is, to my mind, to distinguish clearly between our religious right to the land (effective in the spiritual sphere) and the legal-political right (effective within the constraints of history). The first is eternal and relates to the whole of the land of Israel, while the second is conditioned by actual circumstances that may require, as at present, compromises for the sake of other values.

For the remainder of this essay, I would like to elaborate on this last point, as I understand it from a religious Zionist perspective. The Israeli constituency that identifies itself as "religious Zionist" tries to be faithful, simultaneously, to four transcendent values: the Torah of Israel, the people of Israel, the land of Israel, and the state of Israel. Other sectors of Israeli society, or of world Jewry, are characterized by their loyalty to merely one, two, or three of these values; what distinguishes religious Zionists is their loyalty to all four. In practice, this multiple loyalty imposes a heavy burden, with extra obligations, which is to the moral credit of those who so commit themselves. At the same time, great internal tensions are created, demanding difficult choices and compromises—and therein lies the problematic nature of this position. Religious Zionism is at present undergoing a severe crisis. Its roots, as I perceive them, are in its weakened ability to achieve a true harmony or synthesis of the four commitments. As this ideological/moral fabric unravels, an increasing number of people prefer a one-time "sacrifice," that entails forsaking one of these loyalties, to the constant effort to sustain the fourfold identification with its inherent trade-offs. By paying the price of reducing the multiple loyalty, such religious Zionists enjoy greater ideological consistency and some relief from self-doubt; but the other side of the coin is a marked tendency toward extremism, both ideological and emotional. Such a stance will view compromise as a sign of ideological weakness and lack of resolve, something that must be resisted.

The psalmist teaches, "The Torah of the Lord is perfect, restoring the soul" and "the judgments of the Lord are true, they are altogether righteous" (Ps 19:8, 10), yet the Torah's observance by human beings is inevitably partial and imperfect: "Our Father, our King, remember that we are but dust and ashes." Keeping God's judgments involves a constant struggle with conflicts and contradictions, necessitating hard choices.

The Torah not only acknowledges the legitimacy of these conflicts, but it also instructs us on how to resolve them—for example, by distinguishing between commandments which can never be violated, even at the cost of one's life (the prohibitions against murder, idolatry, and incest), and those commandments which may be suspended in order to survive. The Jew who violates the sabbath laws to save another person's life does not relinquish his commitment to hallow the sabbath day; instead, he faithfully adheres to the order of priorities which the Torah imposes on him in a situation of value conflict. And so it is regarding rabbinic decisions in matters of *halakhah* (Jewish law) throughout the centuries, based on a profound understanding of the needs of a particular generation and on a cautiously responsible use of the exhortation: "It is a time to act for the Lord, (for) they have violated your Torah" (Ps 119:126; *Mishnah Berakhot* 9:5).

MULTIPLE LOYALTY

The biblical dispute between the herdsmen of Abraham and those of his nephew Lot similarly presents us with a value conflict requiring a decisive choice. And Abraham's choice is, in fact, directly relevant to the multiple-loyalty problem which religious Zionists confront today. The land, all of it, was promised to Abraham and his descendants (Gen 12:7), and not to Lot, who journeyed with him. Accordingly, Abraham was entitled to ask Lot to return to Haran, once the dispute between their shepherds erupted and necessitated their separation. But, instead, the patriarch chose another course of action: "Let there not be strife between me and you, and between my herdsmen and yours, for we are brethren. Is not the whole land before you? Please, separate yourself from me—if you will go to the left, then I will go to the right; and if you choose the right, then I will go to the left" (Gen 13:8–9). Abraham was convinced that making peace between brethren took precedence over the immediate exercise of his own right to the land, and for the sake of peace he even gave Lot first choice of territory within the geographic boundaries promised to him by God. Lot naturally took advantage of this extraordinary generosity, choosing the most fertile grazing land along the Jordan River.

One could justifiably ask whether this "territorial compromise" was the right choice for Abraham to make. The biblical text itself gives a clearly affirmative answer. For immediately after Lot goes his own way, God reappears to Abraham and promises the entire land—"northward, southward, eastward, and westward"—to him and his descendants forever. Not only did his temporary concession not undermine his eternal right, but because Lot associated himself with sinful Sodom, his domain was destroyed with the cities of the plain, and his inheritance (and that of his children) was transferred to what became the territories of Moab and Ammon on the eastward side of the Jordan River (cf. Gen 19:37–38).

The Kotzker Rebbe is reported to have said: "There is nothing so whole as a broken heart." By this he meant to teach us that, for anyone whose heart remains unbroken, because he avoids the anguishing choices presented by the clash of *positive* values, such "wholeness" of heart is really an illusion, whereas for someone whose heart is broken, because his love for God causes him to hate evil and refrain from sinning (Ps 97:10), and so he is compelled to make painful compromises and concessions, the breaking of his heart is its very mending. And this is precisely the painful question which brings us to a fateful decision: Does excessive loyalty to the land of Israel, expressed by refusal to countenance territorial compromise, reinforce or undermine the three other loyalties—to the Torah, to the people, and to the state?

The divine commandment to Abraham to "go forth" (Gen 12:1) shows how profound a value the land of Israel is in the Torah; and the "wholeness of the land" is, for a Jew like myself, a religious principle as old as the covenant between the pieces (Gen 15). However, translating this principle, under current circumstances, into a concrete political objective with absolute, uncompromising religious sanction inevitably violates the wholeness, or integrity, of the Torah. Principled rejection of any territorial concession in the service of peace requires, for its practical justification, the refusal by our Arab neighbors to reach a peace agreement with Israel. Arab extremism reinforces Jewish extremism and makes it easier for some to blame the Arabs for perpetuating the hostility and bloodshed. Thus the advocates of "the whole land of Israel" are not at all interested in encouraging Arab moderation, for that would require a parallel moderation on the Jewish side. They brand every expression of Arab willingness to negotiate peace with us a deceitful trick meant to trap and defeat us. In religious terms, this attitude is tantamount to believing that no peace is possible until the coming of the messiah. In the meantime, the only religious obligation, according to this view, is to fight for Israel's survival against her enemies. Imperatives such as "justice, justice you shall pursue" (Dt 16:20) or "seek peace and pursue it" (Ps 34:15) are considered messianic ideals for some future era.

The religious-nationalist refusal to countenance any territorial compromise in the here-and-now results in serious compromises in the moral sphere. By regarding the pursuit of justice and peace as a messianic program for the future, other ethical commandments—like the preservation of human life created in the divine image, or compassionate treatment of the "stranger" in our midst—are given very narrow halakhic interpretations. More universalist understandings of these commandments are dismissed as "humanistic" misconceptions imported from the secular, liberal culture of the west.

A necessary part of any religious Zionist standpoint, including its educational commitment toward the younger generation, is the application of these basic ethical teachings within the Torah to our present situation. That means ensuring the full civil rights and economic equity of the Arab citizens of Israel, as well as striving toward a negotiated settlement with the Palestinians outside the borders of our state, to guarantee the freedom and self-determination of both peoples. Religious Zionism demands a constant commitment to realizing the biblical promises, while taking every precaution to minimize wrongdoing or injustice. Our sages have taught us that a *mitzvah* (commandment) that is fulfilled by means of transgression cannot be called a *mitzvah;* it fails to sanctify the divine name and retards, rather than advances, the process of redemption.

The Crisis of Palestinian Christians

Fr. Peter Du Brul, S.J.

Palestinian Christians are living through a critical phase of their history. This essay aims at describing the major tensions of that phase and the transformations that are occurring. The aspect of the crisis which most interests us is the transformation whereby the crisis of Palestinian Christians develops into the confidence of Christian Palestinians. Although this sounds like a slogan, the shift from being a Palestinian Christian to being a Christian Palestinian is a shift of awareness and responsibility that not only affects the person and community in their self-perceptions, but affects their ways of perceiving and working with others. It is but one of the transformations in process.

In order to focus on these transformations, we must first present the Palestinians in their general and specific contexts before outlining the field of internal tensions in which they live. These first two parts of the essay can be likened to an uphill climb. We will then be in a position to describe more fully some of the external tensions in Palestinian Christian attitudes toward Israelis, and we will conclude with some observations on needs and priorities. These last two parts are more like a descent down the other side of the hill.

1. THE CONTEXT OF THE CRISIS

The general context of the crisis of Palestinian Christians is vast and complex:

—The historical horizons are fixed by the breakdown of the Ottoman empire, the two world wars, the years of the League of Nations mandates in the Middle East, the gradual or violent decolonizations, the emergence of the Arab states and a Jewish state in their midst, the entrance of the third world into international life, and the more recent revival of Islamic political affirmation.

—Such a context must include within its view the geographical and strategic interests of the "great powers": the currents of American, European, and Soviet influence in regional Arab and Israeli politics, economics, culture and ideology

—It must also and especially refer to the other circles of religious faith—the Muslim and Jewish communities—as well as to the circles of secularized Muslims, Jews, and Christians, difficult though they may be to define; for although they find little or no meaning in the religious obligations of those religions, they are barely recognized as "non-believers" by their own communities. Whether they are "no longer" religious, or only "occasionally" religious, they are a real indicator of the kind of context in which "religious" people live.

But these histories, geopolitical powers, and religious or secular circles are only in the background of this essay. In the foreground are the people who concern us: the West Bank Palestinian Christians who accept this identification, who recognize the crisis they are involved in, and who sense the challenge inherent in the possibilities of their growth and transformation. We must have some grasp of their numbers, their geographical and denominational distribution, and their specific context, before we can appreciate the tensions that are internal to their communities.

The Palestinian Christians are not very numerous. In an overall population of 725,000 West Bank Palestinians, the native Christians may number no more than 3.5%—some 25,000 to 30,000 souls, and the resident foreign population may number 1,500. If we add East Jerusalem to the West Bank (as Arab East Jerusalemites, West Bankers and all Palestinians do, despite the Israeli annexation in 1967), we must add 12,000 Christians to the sum, giving us a total of 37,000 Christians in these occupied territories. In Gaza there are about 3,000 Christians. The Israeli Central Bureau of Statistics reported that Christians in 1987 numbered 102,000; this figure refers to the Christians within the borders of the state, excluding the occupied territories, but including East Jerusalem. The following table gives us a fairly exact picture of the number, proportion and distribution of Christians across the land:

	Christians	Muslims	Jews	Druze, others
1. Israel	90,000	615,000	3,611,000	75,000
2. East Jerusalem	12,000	115,700	Included in 3,611,000	
3. West Bank	25,000	700,000	70,000 (settlers)	
4. Gaza	3,000	650,000	13,000 (settlers)	
Total	130,000	2,080,700	3,611,000	75,000

It is disputed whether the Catholics or the Orthodox Christians are in the majority. Assuming that there is a majority, it is not a great one. Since the Greek Catholics have recently claimed to be more numerous than the Greek Orthodox thereby making the Catholics the majority, it is an uncontested fact that the "oriental churches" in our area are more numerous than the "western churches"—even though the Roman Catholics, or "Latins" as they are called locally, comprise as many as 25,000 members. Although this may sound confusing, it is already clear that one cannot speak of numbers without getting into some of the difficulties. These difficulties are based in real differences: between east and west, between Catholic and Orthodox (not to mention the various Protestant beliefs), and the sensitive issue of the Hebrew-speaking Christian communities as separate from the Arabic-speaking communities. Thus languages and rites, beliefs and community loyalties, historical and cultural perceptions of geography are all intertwined. Yet this very complexity gives the community its vitality.

For those interested in seeing the Christian communities in even sharper focus, we present here a table that appeared in the article, "Chrétiens arabes de la Terre Sainte" by Fr. Rafiq Khoury, published in the French monthly *Etudes* in October 1988. The figures in the article are slightly less than the figures already quoted; they are presented as estimates, due to the difficulty of having more precise figures.

CATHOLICS:	Israel	Jerusalem	West Bank/Gaza	Total
1. Greek Catholics	29,000	400	2,200	31,600
2. Latins	16,000	4,800	9,200	30,000
3. Maronites	3,800	50	50	3,900
4. Armenian Catholics	200	200	—	400
5. Syrian Catholics	30	70	150	250
6. Coptic Catholics	20	40	—	60
7. Chaldeans	20	—	—	20
TOTAL:	49,070	5,560	11,600	66,230

ORTHODOX:	Israel	Jerusalem	West Bank/Gaza	Total
1. Greek Orthodox	33,000	3,400	16,500	52,900
2. Syrian Orthodox	50	200	1,700	1,950
3. Armenian Orthodox	300	1,200	100	1,600
4. Coptic Orthodox	500	200	200	900
5. Ethiopians	100	100	—	200
TOTAL:	33,950	5,100	18,500	57,550
PROTESTANTS:				
1. Anglican	500	250	1,150	1,900
2. Lutherans	150	450	1,150	1,750
3. Others	400	300	150	850
TOTAL:	1,050	1,000	2,450	4,500
GRAND TOTAL:	84,070	11,660	32,550	128,280

Notwithstanding the relative accuracy of the above figures, the Palestinian Christians do not think of themselves in terms of such numbers, but as a religious minority, composed of various historical denominations, which take on importance, or lose importance, depending upon the nature of the occasion or the challenge. They are living one of the many forms of Mediterranean Christianity, divided though they may be into various denominations, with different liturgies, customs, loyalties, and calendars. Their baptisms, marriages, funerals are not just folkloric ceremonies, but sacramental events that—through the church communities —keep alive their faith in the nearness of the kingdom of God, in the restoration of the image of God, rooted in real persons and families that dwell across the face of the countryside. Their land stretches out across the hilltops and valleys from Jenin and Tulkarm and Nablus to Jericho, Hebron and Latroun. There was a time some forty years ago when that territory stretched from Gaza and Beersheva to Jaffa, Haifa and Safed, within the borders of British Mandatory Palestine. Now it is cut through by the Green Line (the Armistice line defining the borders between Israel and the West Bank of Jordan from 1949 to 1967); but even this Green Line is being made to fade by the extension of Israeli military occupation services and its "civil administration" as well as by Jewish settlement.

In this larger population there are Christian villages, dug into the hills, the homes of a Christian peasantry. Christian artisans, merchants, industrialists, businessmen, bankers, teachers, engineers, architects, lawyers, doctors and nurses, civil servants, journalists and writers, politicians, chauffeurs, priests, nuns, as well as workers in factories, shops, and offices, and day-laborers, have been living in the towns and cities, with generations of their ancestors buried in the local cemeteries. In addition to the Palestinian Christians on the land, and under the land, there are those who have emigrated. Members of the family can be found in Australia, Chile, California, and Belgium; throughout eastern and western Europe and the Soviet Union; in Algeria, Tunisia, Libya, Egypt and Morocco; in Greece and Turkey; in Kuwait, Saudi Arabia and the Gulf States; in India and Pakistan. Some are studying or working abroad; others have emigrated permanently, or for the time being. Most Palestinian Christian families have relatives who are in Jordan, Syria, and Lebanon, integrated more or less into the local societies and churches, as much as that is possible. Very few Palestinian Christians live in the refugee camps.

Although sharing in the membership of the various traditional churches of the area, Palestinian Christians differ from all the Christians around them. They differ from the Christians on the coast of Syria and in the mountain villages and cities of Lebanon. They differ from the Christians who live in the towns and cities of the Suez Canal, the Nile Delta, and Upper Egypt, and from those who live in the Tigris and Euphrates Valleys. They differ less from the Christians of Trans-Jordan, although they are divided from them both geographically and politically by the Jordan Valley and military borders. The specific context of Palestinian Christians is that they live near the "holy places"; for them, the "holy land" is home. These holy places and the pronounced international Christian presence that surrounds them, in addition to the creation of the state of Israel and to the forces of Israeli military occupation and settlement, give to the Palestinian Christians of the West Bank (as well as to those in Gaza and in Israel itself) a context different from that of the other Christian minorities of the Middle East. This situation keeps the West Bank Christians on the ridge of mountains which the Israelis, since the coming to power of Menachem Begin as prime minister in 1977, have once again begun to call by their biblical names: Judea and Samaria. In the towns and villages across the Green Line, along the coastal plain and in the Galilee, and especially in the cities of Haifa, Nazareth, Acre, and Jaffa, are their "Israeli Arab" Palestinian brothers and sisters.

Besides their geographical and political isolation and diaspora, their living in the "holy land" gives their life together both a certain poignancy, and an irony, shaping the special nature of their challenge. For the "holy land" *moves;* it moves through the "holy time" of the cycle of feasts that keep reminding them of the events of their religious identification and liberation. To this religious calendar another set of dates has clustered into a calendar and an agenda of its own: the Palestinian national calendar of historical events, ranging from the Balfour Declaration of 1917, to the U.N. partition of Palestine in 1947; from the massacre at Deir Yassin and the defeat of the reactionary Arab armies in 1948, to the massacre at Kafr Qasim during the Suez War in 1956; from the Israeli occupation of Gaza, the West Bank, and the Golan Heights in 1967, to "Land Day" in 1976, when six Israeli Arabs protesting land expropriations were shot dead by Israeli troops.

In addition to these national events, the dates of the founding of the various Palestinian political parties are commemorated. The "Intifada" or Palestinian uprising, which began on December 9, 1987, will no doubt be commemorated on that date into the future. Meanwhile the Muslim and Jewish religious calendars move along through the feasts of their cycles, and the Israeli national calendar has a cycle of its own, which links more or less strongly at times with the religious calendar. As their religious feasts go by, amidst the coming and going of other commemorated dates and events, some Palestinian Christians are growing aware of the challenge and the possibilities that their faith implies—not to draw the pity or commiseration of others to their situation, but to draw inspiration and energy for themselves, to harness the energy into working against the forces that deny them, and to empower themselves by trying to maintain a rate of energy production and transmission.

Of course, we are not speaking of "power plants" nor even of transistors, but of communities with faith in the meaning and value of who Jesus was and what he lived for. Their small number is complex, not only because of the many denominations composed of both native and foreign Christians, but because the specific context of their implantation and inculturation in the holy land—under Israeli occupation—exposes them to unique pressures; these social, political, economic, psychological and religious pressures are leading them to break through the traditional attitudes, at various levels, and to create new options, depending largely upon the areas in which they live. It is this breakthrough which especially interests us, but due to the oppressive situation it is difficult to assess it: What *is* really happening to this people? How can they express what is happening to them? With whom can they communicate? In addition to the religious calendar of feasts, and to the political calendar of events, there are other events in recent history which have helped Palestinian Christians to gain a sense of their specific presence and possible role within the situation.

A few such events, which seem to have had a profound impact on their generations, are the visit of Pope Paul VI to the holy land in January 1964—a visit which took him to both Jordan and Israel; Pope Paul's ecumenical gesture of returning the relics of St. Saba to the Greek Orthodox community in the Holy Land in 1965; the foresight and initiatives of the apostolic delegate, Msgr. Pio Laghi, in the years following the Six Day War of 1967; the voice of Msgr. Hilarion Capucci, vicar of the Greek Catholic Patriarchate of Jerusalem, who was accused and convicted of smuggling arms into Israel in 1974, and who spent two years in Israeli prisons before being released on special conditions; the nomination of Msgr. Michel Sabbah, a native Palestinian (from Nazareth), to the Latin Patriarchate of Jerusalem in 1987.

There are other events and movements which may prove to be as significant as the above, such as: the election of the Greek Orthodox patriarch, Diodorus, in 1986; the increasing commitment of Palestinian Christian professionals, students, and workers to the development of social, economic, and political movements and unions; the emergence of new spiritual movements and communities from abroad, and the transformation of some of the older holy land institutions into new centers of academic and spiritual activity. The point we make here is that within their specific context, and in a modest way, Palestinian Christians have a calendar—if not an agenda—of their own. Their contemporary history is less in the process of being written than in the process of being made—or unmade; for, as we said from the very beginning, they are living a critical phase of their history.

It is questionable whether this small, complex community of Christian churches may be central to determining the future of Palestine and Israel. As Christians, they may really be marginal to the problem; their lives will be affected by the outcome of the crisis, but the trend of the crisis will probably not be affected by them. Nevertheless, they are there, in the borders of a Jewish state or under its military occupation, together with a large Muslim majority of fellow citizens, who are Palestinian in origin, but are now legally Jordanian or Israeli, depending on those governments' policies. Like both Muslims and Jews, they are faced with the increasing polarization of their own numbers. The Christians, however, are living through a crisis that questions their very existence in their country, and that challenges them to live through this crisis as Christians.

Both the crisis and the challenge can be summarized in the phrase already mentioned: Palestinian Christians are faced with the challenge of becoming Christian Palestinians, and some of them are responding to that challenge. In other words, there is a tension of priorities and identifications that is gradually, in some cases, undergoing reversal or transformation. In a general and intuitive way, Christians had thought of themselves first as Christians, and then as Palestinians; as pressures have mounted over the years of Israeli occupation, many Christians have grown to consider themselves first as Palestinians, and only secondarily as Christians.

But with time some of these Palestinians have discovered the importance of bringing their Christian values to their Palestinian struggle for freedom and human rights. As this transformation takes place, a new element appears within the crucible of the Israeli military occupation of the West Bank: the trial of Jesus becomes recognizable. The trial of unrecognized, rejected men and women reopens, at the most inopportune of times. And with each new twist of events, as the trial presses toward its close, and as the religious and political aspects of the challenge grow more clear, it becomes all the more urgent to see where one stands, and to what degree one is implicated in the events at hand.

Why is this transformation so delicate and urgent? Because the Israelis, by their oppression of Palestinian Christians and Muslims (insofar as that oppression is perceived by Christians), have unwittingly stepped into the role of some of the Jewish leaders in the gospel archetype. For Christians identify themselves with Jesus, and as they inculturate themselves through history, they have tended to discover and celebrate a Christ who corresponds to their own historical struggles. There is a Greek Christ and an Italian Christ, a Russian Christ and a Latin American Christ, a black African Christ and an Indian Christ, a Chinese Christ and a Polynesian Christ. As these aspects of the Christian struggle emerge from within their various cultures, the forces against which they struggle can also be identified within the scriptural archetype: Roman leaders, Jewish leaders, Judas, Peter, and their own sinfulness.

As Christians of the Middle East have come to inculturate their Christianity in the modern phase of rising nationalism, they find that among the several forces that they are struggling against, there stands the Jewish state. Although centuries have passed, these Arab Christians and especially the Palestinian Christians find themselves—not as Christians, but as Palestinians—oppressed by the Jewish leaders. They are a hair's breadth from identifying this generation of Jewish leaders with those who collaborated in the death of Jesus at the hands of the Roman occupiers.

It is true that Catholic and Protestant churches have clearly stated that all Jews today are not to be held responsible for what some Jews once did, nor were the Jewish leaders then the only ones responsible for the death of Jesus. The clearest statement of this was made in the document *Nostra Aetate* formulated at the Second Vatican Council. But as Palestinian Christians draw upon their faith in Jesus Christ, in their present situation they can appreciate the irony, the uniqueness, and the depth of their situation, as can no other Christian people in the world. They are not just challenged to submit to the trial, and to find consolation in the pity of others, but they are challenged to find an active way *through* the trial—to find in their faith in Jesus the very intention which inspired him to reach out toward all, at the same time that he discerned good from evil, hypocrisy from honesty, and betrayal from loyalty, offering his life for the sinners, but not for the sins.

Whereas, in western Christian circles, there is increasing interest in the Jewishness of Jesus, among Palestinian Christians (and to a lesser degree among other eastern Christians) there is an increasing experience of Jewish oppression. There is also a certain resistance to and suspicion of the idea of the Jewishness of Jesus among eastern Christians. It is true that the Israeli government has gone out of its way to assure strictly religious rights—such as guaranteed access to the holy places, etc.—but these religious rights are only part of a range of human rights that Palestinians need in order to survive as a people, and not just as religious minorities. For they are just as deeply Palestinian as they are Christian or Muslim, and this—for most Israeli policy—is inadmissible.

It is a Christian perception which sees in this situation of the Palestinians a further "trial of Jesus," but precisely because the oppression is coming largely from the Jewish state of Israel, Palestinian Christians are challenged to find in their faith a new way of speaking of Jesus, a new christology, that will be equal to the new situation; for to fall back into the old stereotypes would be to reopen wounds that it has taken centuries to heal, if they have been healed at all. This gives us all the more reason to try to discern what is happening among Palestinian Christians. They are small in number, complex in their denominations, both integrated and scattered in their geographical distribution, inheritors of a unique history in the holy land, and exposed to specific contemporary pressures. They are living through a critical phase of their history that they may, or may not, survive.

Thus far, however, we have only taken a bird's-eye view of our subject in its multiple contexts. As one approaches to get within hearing range of those who live in their homeland, one begins to notice the internal and external tensions which are the theme of this essay. Our readers are presumed to be interested in the relations between Christians and Jews, but it is impossible to understand how and why Palestinian Christians react and respond as they do if one has not tried to understand more about the tensions in which they live. Thus, before we make certain observations about the external tensions between the religious communities, we must briefly indicate the various tensions that are internal to the Christian communities themselves.

2. INTERNAL TENSIONS AND ATTITUDES

In this part of our essay, we are obliged to summarize. But in the following part we will draw upon some of the distinctions which are made here. Three factors are more or less immediately evident: the various denominations of the Christian churches, the foreign and/or local aspects of those churches, and the functional and traditional distinction between clergy and laity, between consecrated religious persons and communities on the one hand and ordinary lay-folk on the other. But there are four other factors that are more subtle, and that are absolutely necessary to understand if one wants to grasp why the external tensions and relations are as they are. These factors are: the place in which one lives, the level on which one works, the attitude toward one's own church, and the options available. We do not intend to present these various factors in detail, but a few observations on each will suggest certain basic orientations meant to forestall misunderstanding.

1. Various Denominations

Although many denominations cluster around the holy places, especially in the Jerusalem area, the great majority of local Christians are members of the oriental churches: the Greek Orthodox Church, and the uniate Greek Catholic (or Melkite) Church. In the West Bank, however, there are few Greek Catholics and many Roman Catholic local Christians; in the Galilee, there are many Greek Catholics and few Roman

Catholics. Gaza's Christian population is almost completely Orthodox. The Armenian community is mostly in the Jerusalem area, whereas the Syrian Orthodox and Catholics are distributed between Jerusalem and Bethlehem. The Maronite church is mostly restricted to the northern Galilee, but was once important in Jaffa. The Protestant churches are to be found in the cities, villages, and towns; their schools and hospitals are highly respected, but Protestants comprise only about two percent of the local Christian population.

This may be the best place to note that these denominations are to be found within both Israel and the occupied territories. But the dominant culture of Israel is that of the Hebrew-speaking Jewish population, whereas the dominant culture of the occupied territories is of the Arabic-speaking Muslim population; it is within and alongside that Muslim population that the great majority of Christians in Israel and in the occupied territories live and work, feel and think.

The oriental churches and the Catholic Church have centuries of experience in adjusting to life within the Muslim world. In Israel, however, in addition to the majority of Arab Christians there, small churches of Hebrew-speaking Christians have arisen. There may be as many as four thousand members of the Messianic Assembly and other Messianic Christian groups, mostly of Protestant origin, and there are about four hundred Hebrew-speaking Catholics. These churches are small indeed, since they comprise only about forty-five hundred people, compared to the total of one hundred and two thousand Christians in Israel and East Jerusalem, but insofar as they are *not* of Arab origin, and have made a deliberate option for Israeli Hebrew-speaking life, they are in a unique position, and experience tensions unique to themselves. They are not accounted for by mere "denominational" categorization. Their members are either Jewish converts to Christianity, or Christians married to Jews, although some of the members are western Christians who work in Israel and who identify with the enterprise of the Jewish state as a necessity for the Jewish people.

Recognition of these Hebrew-speaking Catholics, Protestants, and Messianic Christians makes one all the more aware of the fact that the overwhelming majority of Christians in Israel are Arab Israelis. Although these Arab Israelis (of Christian or Muslim faith) learn Hebrew, they are Palestinians who were forced by a military *fait accompli* to become Israelis or to leave. Palestinian Christians throughout what is now Israel, the West Bank and Gaza lived together in their religious denominations before 1948, and never dreamed, hoped, or expected that some part of them would eventually be called "Israelis," for they are not "sons of Israel." In fact, most Christian children never learn that "Israel" was the second name of Jacob, until they are in secondary school—if then. A political fact is not necessarily a value that one shares, at least at first. And even if one does come to value it—this Hebrew Jewish world, with its positive and negative aspects—it is not usually a value that one could publicly admit to. Why? Because one risks being exploited by the self-justifying propaganda machine of the state.

A final remark must remind the reader that the "holy places" are watched over by the traditional denominations: Orthodox, Latins, Armenians, Copts, and Syrians. With a few exceptions, these holy places are not the parish churches of the local Christians, and are not staffed or maintained by local Christians. This sometimes adds to the feeling among local Christians not only that they are not political masters in their own house, but that they are neither completely at home in their own denominational holy places.

2. Foreign and Local Christians

Because of the international nature of the holy land, with its holy places, its tourist and pilgrim trade, its hotels and other services, its various institutes and schools of biblical studies, theology, and archeology, and because of the many schools and works that have been set up by foreign Christian organizations as a service to the Arab population (of which only about three and a half percent are Christian), local Christians find themselves in the company of a relatively large number of foreign Christians who are in administrative positions.

The two extremes of local Christian feeling toward this situation are that they are either looked after and cared for too much, or that they are overlooked, whereas the Muslims are taking advantage of the offered Christian help. Without harping on the extremes, there is an increasing and probably irreversible move on the part of local Christians to assume responsibility in as many services as they can. There is sometimes a relationship of "double bind" whereby the foreign Christian claims or believes that the local Christian still needs him, at the same time that the local Christian is trying to overcome the fear that, without foreign Christian help and presence, the local Christian will lose a certain status in local Arab society.

There appears to be an over-saturation of foreign Christians in the holy land, since so many of them seem to be there for their own ends, attracted by the land and the events that once took place there, as well as by the contemporary political history of the passage of the holy places and the land under Jewish sovereignty. Increasing numbers of foreign Christians are coming to the holy land in the light of growing concern with the Jewish roots of Christianity. Unfortunately, but understandably, what is positive in that concern is profoundly suspect in the eyes of Arab Christians, whether they are in Israel or in the occupied territories, for they fear that it is only an extension of the enterprise that has divided them.

3. Clergy and Laity

It is understandable that, in view of the holy places and their long history, there would be in the holy land a relatively large number of foreign clerics and religious men and women. The holy land has attracted many missionary groups that have managed to convince some of the oriental Christians (mostly Orthodox) to form the core-group of new churches. These missionary groups are headed by clergymen. Similarly, most of the heads of the various schools and institutes are foreign clergymen. Even in the schools and hospitals and parishes that serve the native Arab Christians, it is often the case that the clergy in charge of them are from Jordan, Syria, or Lebanon. In other words, there have been relatively few local vocations to the clergy and religious life. Despite this, there is a widespread respect for the clergy in the local Christian population, as if stemming from an understanding of the importance of the clerical "buttress" and the clerical services in a Christian society that lives within and alongside a Muslim society.

As Palestinian nationalism has grown and political and cultural consciousness has intensified, the role of foreign clergy has diminished and the role and responsibility of local clergy have reached new and challenging proportions. The Christian communities are in need of leadership, in unprecedented ways. Without attention to the "classical" relationship between clergy and laity, as inherited from centuries of living under an Ottoman system, one can have false expectations of what a "Christian response to the present problems" might be.

4. Levels of Presence and Commitment

Unless one has made the preceding distinctions, the importance of distinguishing the following four levels might be dimmed. For these four levels refer to the levels upon which foreign Christians work among the local Christians, in the occupied territories and in Israel. The fact and the way that they work there, and the power and authority they have, seriously affects the attitudes and options of the local Christians, depending upon the place of their work. These levels help us to situate and evaluate the "level" at which almost all official inter-faith dialogue and lobbying are taking place.

The four levels of foreign Christian presence are as follows:

1. There are those involved in the pilgrim and tourist industries; their clientele is here for a relatively short time, but the administration is more permanent.

2. Others are employed in administering or teaching or doing research in the various biblical, theological and archeological schools for foreign students coming to the holy land. These "schools" include the many centers for spiritual and theological renewal. Again, the staffs are more permanent, and perhaps thoroughly so, but the students stay for several months, a year, or perhaps more. Retreat houses and rest houses are included here.

Both of the above are basically administered by foreigners for foreigners—for everyone from the doctoral student to the "package-tour pilgrim," from the personal searcher to the seminary professor on a sabbatical.

3. A third level can be defined as the level of the local people—Christians, Muslims, or Jews. Some foreigners come to live among them, but by living a form of contemplative life. They are not there primarily to receive pilgrim guests or to educate or care for the sick, but to pray and deepen their own spiritual lives as a form of witness in the "holy land." They learn whatever they need of the local languages in function of this, although the learning of a language is an option to enter into the values and problems of a particular cultural world, with its orientations. Their service to local people and to foreigners is basically their prayer, although they always need to find some way of earning a living by offering something in the marketplace.

4. Finally there are those foreigners who live and work actively with the local people. This does not exclude contact with the other levels, but—to give an example—daily life on the land with the Palestinians of the West Bank and Gaza, or with the Israeli Arabs of the Galilee, is not the same as life in the "holy land." The "holy land" is like a park, an archipelago of holy places, staffed by costumed monks and friars, indicated by emblems, protected by the status quo, leading—as it were—into an enchanted past. But the state of Israel, the ministry of tourism, and the ministry of religious affairs are one world, and the state of Israel, the ministry of defense, and the military government in Gaza and the West

Bank are another; the Israeli annexations of East Jerusalem and the Golan Heights, and the increasing Israeli settlement in the occupied territories in view of ultimate annexation or a more subtle form of sovereignty, lead into an even harder world, which is still called the "holy land" or "the land of Israel." Foreign Christians working at the other levels are aware of this fourth level, but they have not chosen to live and work there.

This distinction of the various levels of commitment of foreign Christians is made slightly more complex by the fact that some foreign Christians working in Israel among Jews have asked for and received Israeli citizenship, so they are no longer strictly "foreign Christians." Following their vocations and insights, these foreign Christians who are naturalized Israelis seem to represent local Israeli Christians, but in fact the overwhelming majority of Israeli Christians are Arab Christians. Such shifts of level and language reveal that the overwhelming majority are actually an overwhelmed majority; the Arab Christians of Israel are overwhelmed by a small but highly articulate, intelligent and concerned group of Hebrew-speaking foreign Christians who are deeply involved in the international Jewish-Christian dialogue. But their actual base, within the Christian population of the holy land, is slim indeed.

5. Living and Working Place

Since we are speaking of internal tensions, we must recall—in addition to the Golan Heights, now virtually annexed to the state of Israel— the three areas in which Christians are found: in Israel, in Gaza, and in the West Bank. The tensions that are inherent to West Bank and Gaza Christians, insofar as they live under military occupation, are shared fully with West Bank and Gaza Muslims. Socially and politically, linguistically and culturally, Arab Christian and Muslim communities are united and intertwined in a way that the Jewish culture, the Hebrew language, and Zionist nationalism cannot disentangle.

But to return to special tensions that Christian denominations, clergy and laity, foreigners and natives, at various levels of commitment, would experience, we can begin by pointing to the fact that for the nineteen years between 1948 and 1967, the Christian communities and Muslim communities of Mandatory Palestine were divided from one another. The territorial jurisdiction of church denominations had to be fixed accordingly; some religious institutions were closed, others had to adapt to a loss or change of population; as the Israeli military government extended into

Gaza and the West Bank, Christian institutions had to deal with greater complexities with regard to work permits, imports, exports, taxes, and permits of various kinds.

Israeli government support to certain Christian medical and social works in Israel can have no parallel in the occupied territories. If we do not draw attention to this factor within this list of internal tensions, we risk letting the readers understand that the crisis of Palestinian Christians is limited to certain general denominational religious problems and other general problems of Palestinian party politics. It is more complex than that, as we have seen; but it is also more alive and more ambivalent than that, as the last two factors will show. For their attitudes toward their own Christianity and their options or positions toward the present situation show both variety and vitality, and in some instances witness to the transformation which this essay is trying to pinpoint. In these last two factors, we limit ourselves to speaking only of West Bank Christians, though we suspect that they hold true of Christians in Gaza and Israel as well.

6. *Attitudes Toward Their Own Christianity*

There are at least four basic attitudes that one can find: the traditional, the indifferent, the silent or suspicious, and the rediscovered.

1. Tradition. The most widespread attitude is that of the traditional community. For example: I am Orthodox because my family is Orthodox. Or: I am a Catholic because my teachers taught me what it meant. Or: We are Protestants because we chose to be.

2. Indifference. The second attitude is one of naive or more sophisticated indifference, stemming from a real indifference or from fear that denominational differences only divide Christians from one another—at least in conversation. For example: I am Orthodox, but it doesn't really make any difference because we're all Christians. Not only is the distinction between the church and the kingdom of God lost or overlooked in this attitude, but the dogmatic, moral, and historical differences have been submerged for the sake of temporary agreement. Such expressions may only affect indifference in front of those who are of another denomination; among members of one's own community, one might more honestly admit to a traditional attitude.

3. Silence, or suspicion. A third attitude is one of greater concern, and greater fear, that the affirmation and insistence on a Christian identity might separate one socially, politically, and economically from Mus-

lim and secularist Palestinians. This fear is grounded in the fact that for many Muslims and Jews, nationality *is* religion, as it seems to be for many Maronites in Lebanon—not to speak of the Irish, the Poles, and the Sikhs. This attitude is expressed by the example: I am a Palestinian first and a Christian second. Or: I am a Palestinian, and my religion or lack of it has nothing to do with you. Why are you trying to divide us by heightening our religious consciousness? Or, with greater hopelessness and determination: If I have to be either a Palestinian or a Christian, then I'm a Palestinian, and let's be done with it! This attitude is sensitive to any false *or* true difference that might expose one's flank to the enemy's aim—to any words or behavior that would tear the social fabric that unites all Palestinians. That is why this attitude would seem to be expressed by the silence that the subject of religion often meets with.

4. Rediscovery. A fourth attitude is one of a rediscovered confidence (or faith) in the difference that Jesus, his affirmation of the kingdom of God, his founding of the church, and the concrete historical churches make in the life of a person, a family, a community, and the world at large. But this discovery is made only after a person has persevered and passed through the third attitude, or as it is being reached by God's grace which is to be found in the traditional certainty of the first attitude, in the naive or affected indifference of the second, as well as in the darkness, suspicion and uncertainty of the third. This confidence is both a choice and a gift.

The majority of younger people—those under thirty—express the second and third attitudes, crossing the quicksands of indifference or refusal to bring the subject up, except with aggressivity. Older people tend to share the first or second attitudes. This generation gap is not conclusive, however. Some revert from the silence of the third attitude to the traditional and somewhat bigoted confidence of the first. Yet among others can be found that transformation mentioned above: the discovery or revelation that a Palestinian Christian is called to become a Christian Palestinian, to bring deeper Christian values to the fact and struggle of being born a Palestinian, and to work one's way up to a higher form of Palestinian Christianity. In other words, the transformation is not linear but circular; sometimes it is the more religious aspect of one's identity which leads, but at other times it is the more political aspect which is primary, and one has to respect the existential time-lag that it takes for one's whole self to come in to what one chooses to do.

The future of the Palestinian churches depends on the number of people who can authentically live out all of these four attitudes, but especially the fourth which offers a new possibility and dimension to the other three. Older people find considerable meaning in their communal identifications as Latins, Orthodox, Melkites, Syrians, Armenians, Lutherans, Anglicans, Baptists; you have to have lived long enough to see the value of these denominations; you have to have celebrated twenty or thirty cycles of the Christian year, attended at least one generation of baptisms, and marriages, and followed processions to cemeteries of one's parents and friends. These rituals with their roots in the past sometimes flower unexpectedly in the dry soul of the faithful friend, whose loyalty to someone better than himself or herself leads him or her into the "round" of the cycle again, and into the one who dwells at the center of the circumference.

Younger people—even some young Syrians and Armenians, whose peoples are not native to the area—consider themselves Palestinians first, and more or less Christian; they are only remotely related to their specific historical and ethnic denominations, except on ritual occasions. This explains why some young Palestinian Christians are apt to assume the second or third attitudes of indifference or suspicion. Nevertheless, others find considerable self-empowerment when they affirm the traditional attitude, and this makes them the envy of some of their peers.

We can end this presentation of attitudes by saying that they are not limited to denominations, but are found among the clergy and foreign Christians, as well as among local Christians living in other places or areas. The attitudes can also be found among the clergy, with regard to their own denominations and to the laity. They can also be found among foreign Christians, who come to serve on one level and then gradually undergo a transformation with regard to their own attitude. It needs to be said that such a deepening and/or transformation of attitudes toward one's own faith can have profound repercussions on one's attitude toward other faiths, such as Islam and Judaism.

7. Options

Palestinian Christians in the West Bank are deeply involved in the Palestinian national movement, some of them more actively than others; but all are embedded in Palestinian Arab culture, with its various ways of adjusting to the special characteristics of the "holy land," nineteen years of Jordanian annexation, and more than twenty years of Israeli occupation and rapidly increasing Jewish settlement. There is no escape from this involvement, except emigration, and even this is a postponement of facing certain issues and pressures that will reemerge in the new host country.

Faced with the "creeping annexation" of the West Bank, West Bank Palestinians—both Muslim and Christian—are confronted with four options, which form habits of survival. They are temporary, not necessarily permanent options; and one option does not always exclude another. In economic affairs one may be forced to choose in one direction, while in political matters one opts in another direction. It is by living under such pressures, and by maintaining one's existence in a field of such options, year after year, that the Palestinians have developed a national and cultural character that has still not been objectively assessed. The four options are emigration, acquiescence, adjustment, and resistance.

1. Some emigrate, in the hope of finding a "normal life" elsewhere.

2. Some admit to powerlessness, either in a religious form of fatalism, or in a "realistic" appraisal of economic necessities and/or of the determining role of the super-powers.

3. Some use what power they have to adjust to the situation, guarding their identities as best they can, but without having much of a strategy to change the situation. They "ride" the situation as if it were a wave that will break, convinced that what is evil will eventually destroy itself.

4. Some resist, violently or non-violently, not only by guarding their identities, but by fighting and working to change the situation to their own advantage. Resistance can take various forms, from narrowing one's vision and energy to the limits of the family, clan, class, or religious group, to committing oneself to the militant political cells of the various parties or movements.

Interwoven among these four options are certain traditional attitudes, ranging from feudal and monarchical loyalties in the villages to more subtle strategies in view of ultimate sovereignty, to be reached with the support of international powers. Christians and Muslims are not just caught in these pressures, like scapegoats, but they have to operate and survive within them, and sometimes in fact they apply pressures of their own, not just out of their common interests, nor out of their attachment to what some call "merely sociological forms of religion," but with real confidence in the transcendence of the values of their faiths, to which they sometimes give themselves with considerable unselfishness and heroism.

In order to better understand the interaction of this field of options, we may be helped by the following example. In a psycho-sociological study in the history of science, it was shown that scientists *tend* to take positions toward a new discovery that depend upon two variables: whether they have a high or low identification with their peers, and whether they have a high or low role inside or outside the group in question. The historical case studied was that of the discovery of electromagnetism, and the various positions that physicists took toward it initially. The discovery appeared to be an anomaly, and four positions emerged: some banned it, some embraced it, some assimilated to it, others adjusted to it.

1. Those who had a low role, but a high identification with the group, tended to ban it.

2. Those with a high role, but a low group-identification, tended to embrace it.

3. Those with a low role and a low identification with the group tended to assimilate to whatever the present situation demanded.

4. Those with both a high role and a high group-identification tended to adjust to the new discovery.

We can adapt this pattern to better understand the situation of religious communities and their attitudes toward the various realities that can be expressed in the terms of "creeping Israeli annexation," "creeping Jordanian confederation," and "creeping Palestinian autonomy and independence." Most laity have a low role within their churches; most clergy have a high role, and a high identification with their denominations. Foreign Christians tend to have a high role, but as Palestinian nationalism increases they tend to have a lower group-identification, even if they sympathize with the goals of Palestinian autonomy and independence. The traditional churches with high profiles, with a high sense of group-identification, and with highly articulated roles tend to have the ballast to adjust to the new situations. Persons with low roles within their religious communities and a low sense of identity with them tend to drift —perhaps even from one community to another. Those native Christians with a strong sense of their individual importance but a low sense of group loyalty tend to be the means or agents used by foreign churches that want to set up a base in the holy land.

This psycho-sociological pattern might prove to be helpful in order to show how the previously outlined attitudes of tradition, indifference, suspicion, and rediscovery can interlock with the options of emigration, capitulation, adjustment, and resistance. Whether or not that is the case, no one can seriously approach an understanding of Palestinian Christian attitudes toward other religious communities if the tensions within the Palestinian community are not understood to some degree. These tensions are expressed in the attitudes and options we have outlined; they depend upon the geo-political situations in which the communities are found; they are inflected by the various levels of foreign Christian presence; they are profoundly conditioned by the denominational diversity with its historical roots, and by the special intertwining of foreign and native Christians among both the clergy and the laity, but especially among the clergy. We are now ready to present the more external tensions with which Palestinian Christians live—tensions that they experience in their relationships with Jews.

3. EXTERNAL TENSIONS AND TRANSFORMATIONS

The Jews, like the Palestinian Christians, are not just a monolithic bloc. We have been dealing with tensions internal to the Christian community, and now that we begin to step out of that subject to face more external tensions, we must not forget that the Jewish community (like the Muslim community with whom Arab Christians live more closely, as within one people) is also criss-crossed with internal tensions. We might consider the languages spoken among the Jews here, their identity problems, their faith and practice, their clergy and laity, their denominations, their "double bind" that exists between eastern and western Jews, as well as between Israeli Jews and the Jews of the diaspora, as well as between religious and secular Jews. In the West Bank, however, except for Jerusalem, the Jews are living in their self-enclosed settlements which have been set up in defiance of international law and opinion. As these settlements thicken, establishing their own access roads and utilities, as well as their own economic base and civilian defense forces, they intend to eventually encircle and enclose the Arab towns, villages, and lands that once encircled them. Until the second or third month of the Palestinian uprising, Israelis who did not reside in the West Bank crossed into it regularly for their shopping, work, and holidays, just as if they were "at home." How often, in the valleys of the Judean desert, did one meet troupes of backpacking school kids on holiday—accompanied by older boys with their automatic rifles! It may be asked: What are the Palestinian Christian attitudes toward these Jews, or Israelis, insofar as they come into contact with them, and from within a conception of themselves that differs almost completely from the idea that Israelis have of them?

To ask such a question, in such a way, is to ask the wrong question. For it isolates the religious factor from the linguistic, social, cultural and historical fact that the Arab Christians are embedded in and enlivened by their own adjustment to the Arabic and Islamic culture in which they have been living for over thirteen hundred years. Secular forms of nationalism—of which Zionism is one—are barely three generations old, within the Middle East. Individual persons and groups might be deeply committed to such nationalisms, but various levels and ranges of society need time to assimilate and to adjust to such new values. There *are* specifically Christian Palestinian attitudes and options toward Jews, but there are two grave oversights that must be avoided. One must not forget that Palestinian Christians are profoundly conditioned by their cultural history and situation in the Arab and Islamic world, and that they are aware of this conditioning; indeed, they are constantly reminded of it.

One must not forget that Palestinian Christian attitudes toward Jews, even when negative, are "open," insofar as they recognize the Jewish roots of their Christian faith. But, with no exception I know of, they think that Zionism is a perversion of the promises of the Jewish faith, insofar as it practically has nothing but a subservient place for the non-Jew in the Jewish state. It has taken centuries of conviviality with Muslims for Christians to reach posts of responsibility in the predominantly Muslim states where they live; but in many instances they have succeeded. This generation of Palestinian Christians and Israeli Arab Christians sees little hope of this happening in the Jewish state. With these two facts in mind, we can now outline some of the Christian attitudes toward Jews in this area—attitudes that express tensions that can possibly lead to transformation, if they are addressed with honesty and care.

First, there is a difference in attitudes that depends upon the generation gap. The younger generation of Palestinians, those born after 1948, consider the Jews to be foreigners, intruders, and enemies; the various degrees of enmity depend on whether one is a refugee or not, and on social, economic, political, and religious attitudes in the groups concerned. The older generation of Muslims, Christians, and secularist Palestinians who knew the "Palestinian Jews" who lived in what is now the West Bank and Israel have more developed opinions. But the immigration of foreign-born Jews has been so massive since the 1930s, and the state of Israel has developed so quickly and in such a western way, that the older generation's opinions, based on their experience, are overwhelmed by the anti-Israeli attitudes that were taught during the nineteen years of Jordanian rule, as a state of war remained imminent. The Palestinian fear of occupation by Israel was justified when the West Bank and Gaza were conquered in 1967. Palestinian attitudes have become even more negative during the more than twenty years of military occupation and the avowed intention of many Israelis to push for West Bank autonomy only as a step toward eventual annexation.

It is a part of the traditional attitude to distinguish between Jews and Israelis, and this is sometimes expressed as the distinction between Jews and Zionists. This distinction is more embittered when it is expressed by the younger generation, or by those who have suffered loss. Israelis are enemies, but Jews are not. Israelis are those aggressive foreigners from Iraq and North Africa, from Eastern Europe and America, who have had the military might, the foreign aid, and the political cleverness to take their land from under them and make it into a state, an atomic power, an internationally renowned arms manufacturer, an Olympic contender, and a participant in the Eurovision song competition.

Whereas a Jew is more of a religious and social identity in Palestinian eyes, an Israeli is a political, military, technological and ideological identity. An Israeli is a Zionist with a machine gun; a Jew is a merchant who prays, who has a sense of the pulse of the economy, and who can tell very funny stories—even about himself! Especially about himself! Such stereotypes may have little to do with reality; they may need so many alterations that we despair of the tailor. They may say more about the Christian and/or Muslim "idea" of Jew than they say about the Jew's idea of the Jew. But it takes time, and circumstances, and opportunities for a people to change its stereotypes, and the momentum and pressures of the occupation have not permitted that.

Second, social contacts between Palestinian Christians and Israeli Jews are minimal. Outside the business world to which most Palestinian Christians gravitate, and outside the factories where many Palestinians work, and outside the occasional prayer meeting or inter-religious seminar, there is little contact to speak of. For fear of being dissociated from his fellow Palestinian Muslim, a Palestinian Christian (who has inherited in most instances a sixth sense by which he or she knows how far Muslim-Christian conviviality will let him reach with impunity) often prefers to remain silent; the result of such a dissociation could be both misunderstanding and some form of reprisal. This is the way that most Palestinians want it to be, even if it means a lower standard of living in some respects. For they have discovered that the Israeli usually takes over wherever he pushes his way in, and wherever he is invited in. There are exceptions, but it is as if the Israelis don't know where their limits are, not only in terms of property, borders, and rights, but squarely in the center of the problems of their own identity.

When Palestinians cry out at being stepped on in the process of being Israelicized (or Hashemized), or extruded, and when they react in violent ways, they are called "terrorists." No distinction is made in public opinion in Israel between real terrorism among certain Palestinians and justified outrage of Palestinians at certain Israeli measures and attitudes. There is outrage, anger, and hatred in the hearts of many Palestinians, and Christian Palestinians experience the sentiments that result from suffered injustice as deeply as their Muslim compatriots do. But what happens then, when this hatred and frustration boils in their hearts? Not long ago I heard a Christian Palestinian (or should I say a Palestinian Christian?) pray during the public intentions offered at Mass: Lord, I pray that you do not let my anger turn into hatred. . . .

The irony is compounded by the fact that at the same time that anger and hatred boil in their hearts, there is a guarded admiration among Palestinians for the achievements of Israel, in the fields where Israel expects to be admired: Look at those muscles! There is a grudging respect for Israeli intelligence, in both the psychological and politico-military meanings of the word; there is a respect for Israel's military power and effective use of brute force, coupled with complex legal justifications. The Ottoman system might not always have been as intelligent, but it too knew how to subject and intimidate and exploit populations that it governed. But the Ottoman empire finally passed away, and many Palestinians expect a similar demise of the state of Israel.

Demise or transformation, bankruptcy or loss of national consensus followed by disintegration of some form or another: it *must* happen. When a former Israeli chief of staff can compare West Bank Palestinians to "drugged cockroaches in a bottle," and when the prime minister can look down from the ruins of the Herodian fortress and express his disdain for the surrounding Palestinian inhabitants as "grasshoppers," one can sense the proportions of the underlying tragic hubris, and one is certain of the fall. Many Palestinians believe that if God exists, and if truth and justice exist—the behavior of the state of Israel is often in outrageous contradiction to the best traditions of the Bible that the Jews have carried down with them through history—it is God himself who will correct the Jews. Here that deep sense of fate in Israel's enemies might meet the biblical sense of Israel's suffering for the sins of its own injustice, committed despite all of God's warnings and help. The guarded commercial relationships, the limited social contacts, the constant bureaucracy and punishment that an extended and prolonged military occupation involves—these do little to diminish the hatred of this confinement and the will to be free of such an existence.

Third, in view of the generation gap and the limited social contacts, is there any possibility that this frustration and hatred may yet be transformed? The humiliation of the occupation, the land expropriations, the demolition of homes, the "accidental" shootings, the forced closing or opening of shops, schools and universities, the traffic check-points, the censorship of mail and the press, the military patrols, the one hundred and twenty settlements appearing shamelessly across the countryside, the semi-circle of mammoth housing developments strung around the West Bank within easy access to Jerusalem and Tel Aviv, the grid of roads and other utilities being built to connect the settlements in the West Bank so that they will be as strongly independent as possible—all this is being carried daily, weekly, monthly, yearly in men and women, in young and old, in families, clans, neighborhoods, villages, camps, towns, cities, through Jerusalem, and into the Palestinian society that lives within the borders of Israel and carries an Israeli passport.

In the face of this, the West Bankers have to prove themselves constantly to Palestinians outside the country, to Palestinians inside Israel, to the world at large, and to themselves, as they try to hold on to their lives, their land, their rights, and what remains of their past, as well as their stake in the future. The Palestinian uprising, which began on December 9, 1987, is the most recent and prolonged response to the forces that are trying to suppress them. This situation confronts the values and beliefs that each one has inherited or has come to develop. Like the Muslim, who brings his existence and his complaint to his prayer and reflection, so the Palestinian Christian at certain moments in his life brings his hatred and his love, his complaints and his aspirations, to the places in his own land where Jesus lived and also prayed. The holy sepulchre is right downtown; the garden of Gethsemane is not far away; there is a church in every Christian town; there is a religious picture in every home. But what happens in a person's heart, there at that place, echoing with the shuffling feet of tourists, the explanations of the guides, the whining liturgical chants, and the hammering of the workers restoring the building? Does the hatred dissolve? Does it turn back into anger?

Sometimes when I ask West Bank Palestinians if they see any real future for themselves here, I hear that they do not want to live under anybody anymore. There *is* a real hope to finally live on their land without being under Israeli or Jordanian rule. They want to live in a "state" with Palestinian Muslims who have been their compatriots in the long awakening march that began for them with the end of the First World War and the end of Ottoman rule. They want to have open borders with the states around them, but *they* want to determine the nature of that opening. In a sense, there is already a Palestinian "state"; it is a "state of mind," a state of suffering and a state of response to the causes of that suffering, and it is striking out to give concrete, recognized political borders to that "state."

When I ask if this is realizable, some tell me that this *must* be, for it is their only hope; any other solution would simply be the result of eliminating Palestinian opposition and imposing a foreign will on the local people. Others say, with some cynicism, that such a solution depends entirely on the super-powers, on the U.S.A. and the U.S.S.R., who control the whole regional game. Others say that it *will* be, because history is determined by the forces of production, the workers, whose commitment to the class struggle and eventually to armed struggle will result in the overthrow of the exploiting classes of Palestinians, Israelis, and other reactionary Arab states which are controlled by the international imperialist strategy of the profit-motivated capitalists. Although very few subscribe to such an overly rigid and doctrinaire formulation, the refinements of analysis and adaptation to regional issues are guided by an overall conviction that the Marxist reading is correct. Still others say, with a weary smile or with fierce conviction, that this will be, "If God wills." "*Insh'Allah!*"

This presentation of general attitudes toward the future political solution does not pretend to be exhaustive, nor are the attitudes mutually exclusive, but it provides a framework for the more specific attitudes that we will now outline. The seriousness of the attitudes just expressed depends on the quality, age, depth, and resilience of the relationship between the communicators. But one must not forget that one does not always say to others what one only says to God.

But not all Palestinians are known to pray. The hatred in hearts can be turned against Israel, the neighboring Arab states, the European powers, the U.S.A., the U.S.S.R., and even against oneself. The privacy of this prayer, and the complexity of the hatred of the situation, make communication a matter of intuition, acceptance, rejection—as if one were unwinding bandages from an open-wounded arm. But let us listen to some of the voices. Some are concerned with God, others with Israel; some with foreigners, others with themselves. We number these opinions, only for clarity's sake.

1. The return of the Jews is God's way of punishing us.

2. The return of the Jews is bad for us, but God seems to be with them.

3. God has his plan, and our day will come!

4. These people in "Israel" have nothing to do with the Jews who were here in the time of the Bible, and it is pure propaganda to speak of their "return." The true return or "ingathering" took place once and for all when the Jews returned from the exile in Babylon. That is the event that the prophecies were referring to. The use of such prophecies, coupled with the exodus paradigm from the Torah, is a perverse use of the scriptures to justify a secularist twentieth century state-making operation, which has been accelerated and fueled by the Holocaust.

5. Israelis and diaspora Jewry are simply putting into practice what was written in the *Protocols of the Elders of Zion,* which—even if it is a forgery and a piece of anti-Jewish propaganda—is inspired partly by an observation of the Jewish desire to survive! They realize—like other international bodies—that they have to *be* international to survive, and that at least part of their activities have to be secret in order to be successful. The state of Israel is the twentieth century centerpiece of a strategy of survival and domination in the areas that are strategic to that survival. This might be good, this might be bad; but it is a fact.

6. Israel is nothing more nor less than the creation of international imperialism and its strategic interests; the Zionist enterprise has learned how to make itself indispensable to those interests. It is serving as a policeman in the area, and as an agent for its interests in other parts of the world as well.

7. Israel is doomed, as the French in Algeria, the Americans in Vietnam, and the white regimes in Africa were doomed. The U.S.A. and other friends of Israel will finally abandon it (as some Israelis themselves predict) when Israel finally goes too far and compromises their interests elsewhere.

8. Worst of all are those foreign Christians who support Israel for allegedly "biblical reasons," or who go coolly about their biblical or Jewish studies, but are blind to the transformation of Israel into a state with a growing racist fringe and certain adamant racist seeds in its core. The silence of the churches confronted with this is as immoral as their silence when they were once faced with Nazism.

9. We Palestinians are so divided among ourselves—due to the self-interest of many of our own people, and to our confusion at the many currents that are eating away the land and sense of sovereignty under our own feet—that we cannot focus clearly enough on our real situation.

Instead we have to take for truth the interpretations of the data that are already "pre-cooked" according to party ideologies, traditional socio-religious viewpoints, or romantic revolutionary poetry, soaked in irony on the one hand and tragedy on the other. We are barely permitted to have our own experience, before some other party has claimed it as a "fact" in its system of interpretation. We are being ground down into a "non-existence," into a "non-fact," into a "non-entity." This gives us a unique view of the whole world, if only there were someone out there to tell it to, and someone left in here to tell it. We may be a "revelation," but we're in a sealed envelope.

Such emotion-laden statements are breathtaking, provocative, enervating, even infuriating, or merely banal and outworn, depending on the convictions and feelings of the speakers and listeners. It makes a great difference whether you are the accused, the guilty-bystander, the accuser, the judge, or the executioner. You may just be a witness. And this brings us back to the "trial" and to the heart of the "crisis" (or judgment and decision, option, commitment) which is our subject.

No matter who the listener may be, such statements as those made above tend to discourage the real questions from ever being asked; they stop discussion and communication at its source. Thus, in the next paragraphs we are no longer "outlining" Palestinian attitudes that are expressed, but we are trying to formulate those basic questions that underlie some of the previous attitudes. These formulations are our own, and they can claim to be no more than guesses and approximations of the basic questions.

It seems almost impossible to ask the question: What does the coming of so many Jews and the creation of a Jewish state really *mean* for Palestinians, as a people who are both Muslims and Christians, struggling and wrestling to relate their faiths to their national experience and aspirations? Palestinian Muslims and Christians are tending to become Muslim, Christian, and/or secular Palestinians, but the Palestinian Jews took another way at the crossroads of the 1920s, the 1930s, and the 1940s, and with the help of funds and immigrants from abroad, in the light of a vision confirmed by the Balfour Declaration, and further motivated by the holocaust of European Jewry, and with the help of the levers of control in international bodies, they became Jewish "Israelis."

They carried along with them about 200,000 Palestinian Christians and Muslims and Druze, who are now supposed to be "Israelis" as well. These multiple conversions, however, did not really take place as hoped. And the gradual discovery is that the 700,000 Palestinian refugees who were forced out, or fled in the hope of return, have formed into one of the most militant, persistent and internationally recognized "liberation fronts" of modern times. They have kept alive the hopes of both the "Palestinian Israelis" and the Palestinian West Bank Jordanians, as well as the Palestinian Gazans and the Palestinian diaspora.

Such a statement, with its fading echoes, has to be heard long enough to get a sense of the size of the cave. One has to give the echo time to make its way back. The fundamental problem is that so few people have enough ability, patience, and strength to wait for the answer, and for further questions that can come up from within their own hearts; instead, people tend to react out of fear, putting an end to discussion by repeating the same interlocked set of previously conceived responses. The fundamental problem is that it is so hard for any of us to find that his own rock, or principles, form a "cave" and that God dwells there. If he does not, then an idol has taken his place.

Other questions arise. How can this ingathering of the Palestinians intermesh with the ingathering of the Jews? Is there any profound religious component to this event, or is it just reducible to social, economic, political, historic factors, as the secular ideologies say? Do the years of Palestinian longing and resentment, and the years of exploitation and encouragement by various Arab governments and leftist or rightist liberation groups, have to be demystified? And can the same question be posed, on the Jewish side, with regard to the Holocaust?

To what extent do both Palestinians and Jews have to assume greater responsibility for what happened to them *before* their twin tragedies in the 1940s, without forgetting what is incomparable and unique to each? Was there anything in their behavior in the societies and historical circumstances in which they lived that could have evoked justifiable resentment on the part of the wider population? Did their own short-sightedness cause them to underestimate the evil arising around them? What might have led them to overestimate their ability to deal with the distrust, the hatred, and the perverted ideologies which co-existed with certain religious teachings? Who dares ask such questions, and get out of the forum alive? It is a very delicate situation, daring to ask whether all the victims were always so innocent, and whether they are not still being used to cover up for lost chances of taking responsibility?

Are not the national movements of both Jews and Palestinians an avowal and a proof that they do need to take greater responsibility now, because they hadn't done so—or hadn't been allowed to do so—in the past? Others had taken it for them and from them, and they hadn't objected effectively enough then. Just as Jews might better study the Palestinian past, so Palestinians might better study the Jewish past, without being satisfied by the biased revisionist versions that some of their compatriots publish as propaganda to unify the masses. But it is not enough to study the past, to weigh the bias in the authors, and to fight one's own bias; it is even harder to be fully present to one another now—not to force one's way into another's presence, but to try to be present enough to know where the real gates of admission and recognition might lie.

It is tragic, ironic, and ludicrous by turns to see the enormous energy and intelligence expended by Israelis to gain western and even third world favor, and to maintain it, whereas so little care and respect have been shown for the ways of Arab culture. Now that the majority of Israelis are of oriental origin, one might expect them to be more understanding of the Arabic culture in which most of their parents were raised; but this has not been so. And as Sephardi Jews came to search for ways to power within the Israeli system, it was through the rightist Likud party that they found roads of access.

In the face of this necessary effort to come to grips with conflicting ingatherings and emigrations, with conflicting attitudes of powerlessness, adjustment, and resistance, do Palestinian or foreign Christians here have anything specific to say about this, or is their silent presence a specific contribution?

Does this transformation from being Palestinian Christians to becoming Christian Palestinians permit either the Palestinians or the foreign Christians to be silent, or does it rather require a new language and assurance, a new way of searching and affirming, of refusing, of addressing one another, and of acting together?

Is it possible that each side is trying to reach the other, like one hand that is trying to find the other? Could it be that the hands are wrestling with one another, and do not know that they belong to the same body?

Although there are many other important questions, leading deeply into historical and contemporary issues, in matters of great political, social, and economic importance, we think that the above questions have to stand, and cannot be swept under the table, because they underlie so many of the real attitudes that we have outlined above.

4. A CONCLUSION ON NEEDS AND PRIORITIES

It is said that tensions are only a normal part of life, and that life is made up of them. The interwoven lives of communities witness constant tensions and resolutions, including those tensions that become so intense that communities and individuals, minds and bodies, break down. Some "resolutions" are so constant that they take the name of status quo. But the tensions we are addressing are definite signs that the Palestinian Christians are alive, even though they might not be very strong. Is this life growing, and giving more life, or is it dying? The answer would seem to be that something is definitely dying, and something more definite is coming to be born. But fear grips this pregnancy, and truths labor to be born in heated conversations that are never completed, and never written out to allow more objective reflection.

Perhaps some truths will never withstand expression in words, except in a humble and indirect way, and can only be lived out and witnessed to in the relations where true friendship exists. But I think that such a position on the inexpressibility of truths is a "cop out," an escape from the real labor and pain that must be gone through. It is to be hoped that this living, articulate witness to the truth, and this daily refusal of a life that is a lie, or just a game, will be penetrated by the grace that emerges under pressure, so that a better life and sovereignty in the body of the Palestinian community might at last be born, and come into a fuller existence. For, until it does so, and thereby assumes fuller responsibility for itself, others will be assuming responsibility for it, and maintaining it in a state of subservience that it cannot but resist—and resist violently, unless it is forced into positions of powerlessness, assimilation, and adjustment.

Palestinian Christians hope not only to live in their society (and have free access to their "holy places"), but to rule together with their people, to reach sovereignty, to have dominion. This is to fulfill the basic commandment in Genesis, when God created man and woman, "to increase and multiply, to fill the earth and subdue it, and to have dominion" (1:28). That the Jews from whom came this tradition on the meaning and purpose of life should—as Israelis—be keeping them from reaching sovereignty is not just a fundamental irony of the situation, but a sign that Israeli Jews themselves have strayed from the justice of their own tradition. Israel's wrestling with the Palestinians is a "midrash" on Jacob's wrestling with the angel; after the night of their struggle, Palestinians really have something to say that Israelis need to hear.

An equal irony, and injustice, is that the Palestinians have proved no better at keeping the commandments that God gave on Sinai and in Moab. But Muslim Palestinians don't accept or recognize the "biblical" version of God's word as the final version, for that is found only in the Quran; and secularist ex-Muslims and post-Christians don't believe in any version of religious traditions. Christian Palestinians who do accept the Bible in both its "Old" and "New" Testaments have almost no instruction on how to understand and interpret, in the light of modern scholarship and of the church's pastoral teaching, the very texts that Jewish and Christian Zionists use to defend the legitimacy of a Jewish state in the holy land.

There are no "guidelines" from the Christian hierarchy in the east on such burning issues, although "guidelines" are issued in the west on how Judaism is to be presented in Christian catechetics so that the monster of antisemitism will not be unleashed in a new generation. One of the ironies, and even tragedies, of our time is that the creation of the state of Israel may have done more to unleash antisemitism—or at least anti-Israeli feeling and consciousness around the world—than any previous historical instance of Jewish behavior. This was not intended, one can say, as one can also maintain that such a "stage" has got to be gone through. There remains the fact that in the international forum, Israel is a "whipping boy," though at other times it is the P.L.O. which must be excoriated by "all civilized nations." Verbal whipping, however, and even the occasional but persistent act of violence aimed at Israel, are met with the brute force and "intelligence" that Israel commands at each step of the process; and the process oscillates from the military to the diplomatic solution, from the "international conference" to the "separate peace through direct negotiations," from "limited war" to stalemate and "business as usual."

This embarrassment or sensitivity on the level of the texts and traditions (and lack of "guidelines") is like a nakedness that most Christians prefer to cover up, and not like a nudity that they can accept. Yet it is the very place from which their own lives came, and from which future life will come, if it comes at all. There is a difference between exhibitionism and modesty, but there is also a difference between fear of the truth and love of the truth. There is a moment of revelation, in the eye of the storm, where exhibition and modesty, fear and love, in the truth are one—provided that one has the courage to reach that point.

The eye of the storm lies in that vital area of our mutual nakedness and vulnerability before one another; it is the turning point within the swirling vortices of our fear and our faith, our infidelity and distrust, our hope and our despair, our hatred and suspicion, our friendship and love, our living and "reigning" or responding and ruling together. Our nakedness is there in the tension of such contradictions, which are reaching for covenant. In the Old Testament the sign of the covenant is the circumcision of the male; in the New Testament it is the bath of baptism and the partaking in community of the body and blood of Jesus. Writing about such a turning point which is at the heart of repentance is to take a risk—and not only the risk of being blown away by the storm, but the risk of reaching that "eye" or center, at least to some small degree, reaching it just long enough to encourage others to reach for it, too, and to let themselves be reached, for no one can reach it or stay there alone.

This generation of people who share their divided lives in the holy land, including the Christian communities, bears great responsibility in bringing that one life through the labors of conception, gestation and birth, or in being willing or unwilling accomplices to an historical abortion. This generation is not there to midwife someone else's labor, and someone else's birth, but it is there to give birth to a new phase of itself. Christians here tend to look for midwives from outside; they look to popes or bishops, to the World Council of Churches, to consulates, embassies or other international organizations. Together with other Palestinians, they look to Amnesty International, the Red Cross, the U.N., the initiatives that come from the socialist or capitalist worlds; they may look for a miracle from God, or "history"—some sign that they will be saved. They have not yet discovered the truth of what Jesus meant when he said that the only sign they should expect is the sign of Jonah. For fear of doing what one believes should be done, one is carried off by the digestive juices in the belly of the whale. Will Palestinian Christians recognize and assume their role in time and be vomited up, or will they be digested by the hungry forces of their situation? By swallowing the West Bank and Gaza, and particularly Jerusalem, in such a way, did the state of Israel swallow the very hook which cuts its mouth and takes its life? Are Christians just part of the hook, or its "point"? A marginal point? Or can they also have the strength to heal? Will they be reborn, or be midwives to the births of others? Will they eventually reach the age when they can give birth to another generation? The confidence that can overcome this fear is the confidence that Jonah himself learned only when he was being carried in that dark belly (Jonah 2).

SOME CONCLUSIONS

We will end this essay by sketching four areas of priority for all Christians caught in this crisis, no matter what their attitude or position, level or place might be. These priorities can be summed up in the following words: persons and groups have to try to understand and evaluate the situation as it really is, so that they can do some serious planning, in the light of a clear vision of the role of Christians in the pressures of the situation. This planning and vision should be especially attentive to what is new and unique to the situation in the holy land.

There should be a greater effort on the part of Palestinian Christian intellectuals, educators, professional men and women, laity and clergy, with the help of sympathetic and critical foreigners, to formulate a view of their situation, from different viewpoints, so that more Palestinians—be they Muslims or Christians, or even Jews within Israel or in the settlements—may come to understand the situation through such efforts at objectification. This takes time; it takes courage to publish such efforts, to approach both the lowest common denominators as well as the more particular and unique numerators. The cross of those who are rejected from society, who are executed outside the walls, is always the lowest common denominator; and insofar as one approaches it, one tends to get a better vision of the whole society which has agreed to such a marginalization if it is to remain as it is, as a status quo that resists transformation.

The question of future recruitment of clergy, of lay leadership, of future administrations of Christian parishes, institutions, services, property, should be raised more faithfully in the local community. Can it be that there are new forms of religious community that should be developed and encouraged? What is to happen to the parishes, schools, hospitals, clubs, associations, services, monasteries? To what degree can the local Palestinian Christians assume more responsibility for them? To what degree must the cooperation between local and foreign Christians be strengthened, or be changed to another basis, or kept as it is? Is there any choice?

How can people develop a deeper attachment to both their Christian religious life and their national life, unless they understand that their Christian life is lived *in* their national life as well: that the church is the concrete historical local, regional, and global institution, or set of institutions, which has the vocation and mission to announce that the "kingdom of God" is near. This "kingdom" is not a "second life" after death, but *this* life, lived from its depths, that passes through death. It is a life lived from that unity of inner faith and outward expression of which Jesus spoke at the end of the sermon on the mount (Mt 7:24) and in his conversation with Peter at Caesarea Philippi (Mt 16:18).

In terms of planning for the future, one must ask when and how Palestinian Christians are going to communicate more substantively with Jewish Christians or "Messianic Jews"? To what degree are the Palestinian Christians called to play a role in the search of Jewish Christians for a place in the configuration of the eastern and western churches? To what degree do political, cultural, and historical differences isolate these two Christian bodies from one another, thereby hindering them from sharing their experience, their difficulties, and their visions of the situation?

The problem of recruitment, or "vocations," brings the local and foreign Christians face to face with the problem of over-saturation of institutions that represent the histories of both eastern and western Christian spiritualities of contemplation and service, in their institutional forms; and it also brings the Christians to look toward the future, and not just toward the Ottoman and colonially dominated past and present. This future-oriented attitude might also relativize the more fatalistic kind of faith that is so widespread, so that more Christians come to understand the risk and trusting commitment that are essential aspects of true faith. The recruitment of Palestinian Christians will not be of much help, however, unless the existing attitudes of some of the clergy and laity face more affirmatively the national problems.

A further agenda item is the formation of groups of committed Christians who can discuss, criticize, and contribute to the development of the problems raised above—namely, realistic assessments of the situation when considered from the viewpoint of living faith, and efforts at formulating a larger vision in which planning for the future can take place. Some of the areas that must be studied and discussed are catechetics for both children and adults, liturgy and the quality of preaching, relations with both Muslims and Jews, deeper relations with more secularist groups in society, and the place of religious studies within the program of general education. Both the secularizing tendency and the interfaith tendencies should be taken more seriously, so that the whole area of religious freedom might assume its true place in the struggle for human rights and for being responsible in the exercise of them.

There is a pressing need for Christian awareness and action in the face of the Israeli military occupation. The emigration of Christians and Muslims, the land expropriations, the conditions of prisoners, the gradual incorporation of utilities like electricity and water into the Israeli grid and pipelines, the complexities in the health, labor, education, and tax spheres —these are common problems, and there is a need for all members of the Palestinian people to become aware of the framework in which these various developments occur; but in addition, and indeed first of all, people have to act.

Fellow Palestinians have a right to expect from Christian Palestinians a behavior, even an analysis of the situation, that corresponds to their name "Christian." Do the name and the belief really make any "difference" in *practice?* This is the question and the challenge that both local and foreign Christians here have to live with.

The national situation does tend to divide, or at least differentiate, Palestinian and foreign Christians on some issues, though it sometimes unites them. The fellow-feeling, the sympathy, are not always matched by similar analyses, opinions, choices. Pressure must come from the local communities so that the patriarchs, bishops, clerical leaders and chronic complainers among the local and foreign laity take greater initiative in protesting injustices and proposing more just measures. But pressure rarely even builds up; the channels or pipes of the mechanism are so scattered, complex, and fearful of risk that only rarely is the energy converted into work and power—and this is mostly done when the issue is property and taxes, or something else that is concretely quantifiable.

Poor communication between the laity and the clergy is perhaps the basic reason for the ineffectual leadership of the hierarchy. The highly discreet forms of protest and proposal that the Christian hierarchy does make are almost completely unknown to the laity at the base, because such communication with the base has rarely been sought. Until recently, it has been a one-way relationship: from the top, down. Dialectically, it is the Israeli occupation that is making this communication more necessary, though at the same time the occupation makes some Christians more fearful that such communication and action would only give the Israelis more of a pretext for interference. The fear cuts both ways. As time passes, the situation grows worse.

There is also the relatively difficult question of improving relations with Jews, as members of their religious communities. It is almost exclusively foreign clerics, working on what we called the "second level" of institutions serving foreign students who are temporarily in the country, who undertake ongoing relations with those Israeli Jews open to interfaith contacts and dialogue. The political situation, in addition to the language problems, makes such relations between local Christians and local Jews both uneasy and suspect. It is rare that local Christians are even brought into contact with the foreign Christians who are "professionals" in Jewish-Christian relations in this country or abroad. It is only insofar as local and foreign Christians move from the attitude of silence to affirmation and discovery that these relations will develop, reach their "critical mass," and break through to new territory, new visions, and the use of new energies that are hidden in the very issues that are so sensitive.

The point is that we are searching for something that is new—something that has not been discovered yet, that is in us, and among us, but has not yet been born. It is not a form of newness that is hidden in the future, but that is hidden in the present, and has been here all along. We are involved in a creative process, growing toward a moment or stage of recognition, of independence, of a new equilibrium and maturity. There must be in us a real hunger to reach that moment—not a lust, not a violence, but a patient hunger to be satisfied with nothing short of it. It is the hunger and thirst for justice mentioned by Jesus in his sermon on the mount (Mt 5:6) that comes from the purity of heart which works for peace, and is willing to suffer for the liberation of the poor, the meek, and the mourning. There must be a sense of the need to break through what is secondary in the "holy land" to find those eternal springs that are really flowing in the holy land; to grasp new interrelationships; to grasp the old hands in new ways, and new hands for the first time; to realize that the problem here is not just another third world problem of national rights and freedom from oppression—another El Salvador, another Vietnam, another Algeria—but a situation which is unique, where those who identify with biblical Israel find themselves faced with twentieth century Palestinians, who are not idolatrous Canaanites but Christian and Muslim monotheists.

Many Christians see profound irony in a certain reversal of biblical roles: insofar as the Palestinians are in bondage to the Israelis, it is the Israelis who have taken over the role of the "Egyptians" in the exodus story, and it is the Palestinians who have the role of the "Israelites"; the irony is compounded by the fact that in contemporary politics, the bondage of the Palestinians has been sealed by the Camp David agreements between Israel and Egypt. In addition to the political and military bondage, there is a form of spiritual bondage, in which we can see both Israel and the Palestinians implicated—each holding the other hostage to a form of fear, of insecurity, of deportation or extermination.

Due to the nature of the Jewish state and the experience out of which it has been created; due to the Arab hostility that the state has met; due to the nature of the Israeli annexations and occupation since 1967; due to the nature of the Palestinian experience of exile, oppression, and fighting to reclaim their land, the same land that the Jews claim to be theirs—we are up against a huge problem, unique, requiring nothing short of a reinterpretation by all of us of our biblical and scriptural traditions. And not a revisionist interpretation, either. Are we really equal to such a challenge? Are we worthy of it? This is what makes a "Palestinian Christian liberation theology" so difficult.

The "classic" Latin American liberation theologies use the Old Testament "exodus paradigm" as the model underlying their application of the "New Testament paradigm" to their particular political, social, and cultural circumstances. Palestinian Christians have a much more difficult task, for their perceived oppressors are the Zionist Jews themselves—at least those Jews and others who believe that Palestinians have no right to sovereignty on this land.

Thus the Palestinian Christians (and even the clergy) tend to shy away from certain parts of the Old Testament, thereby implicitly recognizing that the literal or hyperbolic Zionist interpretations of the Old Testament texts are accurate. They may also feel that they are not equipped to get into textual and hermeneutical discussions, which sometimes appear as complicated as nuclear physics. In addition, the high temperature of fear, anger, and frustration does not often allow for detached presentation of the data and cool discussion of the arguments for possible interpretations. This is one of the major problems. Each time an Arab Christian reads or hears the word "Israel" in the scriptures, he or she must instantly flinch and take the time to distinguish between biblical pre-Christian Israel and later or contemporary post-Christian Israel, including the state of Israel. The Palestinian Christian communities in particular cannot permit those differences to be gummed over; for if they are, it is the Palestinian Christians themselves who are gummed over.

I have heard an American Catholic theologian tell a group of Palestinian Christians that they might have to resign themselves to disappearing from within the Jewish state and the occupied territories. At a Christmas mass in Bethlehem, only three weeks after the Palestinian uprising had begun, a group of foreign Christians was singing a well-known Christmas carol that ends with the phrase: "Born is the King of Israel!" An elderly Palestinian who was attending the mass tightened up for a moment, and then, before the next stanza began, he said in a firm and moderate voice to himself and to those standing close by: "the *new* Israel." It was clear that by this he meant the church.

There is a greatness to the crisis into which we have been born. We may not give much consideration to the fact that we have been created at such a time. We may not see what this can mean for the future. We may not believe that the history of the planet's peoples, in some deep sense, has been aiming at this recognition that we have all been relativized by one another. It is possible that one can so deviate from one's own tradition and "paradigm" that roles are reversed, until they are once again restored. When they are restored, one is no longer the same; a transformation or conversion has occurred to reveal how deeply our lives, and even our deviations, and our corrections, are interdependent. Such relativization and transformation happens, at least for Christians, in the magnetic field of the trial, execution, and resurrection of Jesus. That trial, labor, passion goes on in each age, in the awareness that the age is dying, and a new one is coming to be born. The new Jerusalem descends as the smoke of Babylon rises. Peter weeps as Judas hangs. John stands by and the rest have fled. Jesus cries out and the Temple veil is rent. We may believe that this has happened, but we may not believe that this is happening now, and that tensions can lead not only to breakdown, but to breakthrough. The tension of the cross experience breaks through the whole cloud that the Temple veil represents—the cloud that covered God's words on the journey from Sinai to the promised land. When that cloud-veil is rent, it can only show us what we already heard was there: God's word, which says: "I am." But we can only see that word, in all its nakedness, from that one place where man or woman is completely rejected, and where we ourselves have been willing to give up everything—the place Christians recognize as the cross; the place that Jews today are calling the Holocaust; the place that Palestinians have discovered in the last forty years of rejection and exploitation and struggle. Every person, every people, every age or configuration of peoples, goes through this trial, though he might recognize it in very different languages, symbols, histories, and frames of reference. For him, at least, it will always be a unique experience. But no person becomes a person without it; no people becomes a people without enduring it; no age becomes aware that it is an age—that it is *of* age—without recognizing and confronting it. We are at such a moment in the history of this century; we are at its crossroads. And perhaps we carry our crossroads perspective with us.

The small circle of West Bank Christians would be miserable indeed if it did not know where it stands in the currents of this century, moving with the other circles of the West Bank community, under so many internal and external pressures and forces. Yet the Palestinian Christians are the first Christians, who, as a people, are in daily and yearly confrontation with Jewish people who have stepped out of the traditional "Old Testament" paradigm to carve a state out of the overwhelmingly Muslim Middle East. This is not just a "biblical problem" or curiosity for them; nor is it a distant, "international" political problem; it is as close to them as their money, their bills, their radio and TV stations, their goods, their I.D.

cards, and the heavy dealings with all the complexities of an occupying military government, which protects increasing Jewish settlement on the land.

Palestinian Christians, small and complex though they be, and subject to multiple interior and external tensions, are at the vanguard of having to deal with Jews in a Jewish state—a Jewish state within whose militarily extended borders they exist as a subjected people. As they try to relate to that situation, from various places on the land, they are challenged by a complex task.

Yet amidst all the lamentation, there might be heard from time to time a small word of thanks and praise for having been squeezed in here, to be born to be part of such a time, to be called to take part in it, to be chosen to choose a way through it.

This praise comes from the recognition that we are deeply involved in something new that God is doing in the world, that is not just fixed fatefully in the pattern of what he has already done—although it is figured there. This experience of something new in the Christian communities of the West Bank is a priority, insofar as it is an experience of God *in* this situation, and in us in a new way; it is a recognition that God is *a priori*, that he is ahead of us, that we are catching up with him, that he has his plans and his way of using us, and of asking us more and more freely to let him use us, even though we don't understand how such cooperation is going to work out.

The cooperation of people across religious and national barriers must be based not just on a future orientation, and not just in fidelity to the past, but in this experience of God doing something new *now*, in the present situation. This experience does not add to the tensions already listed, but makes them bearable and leads them toward a transformation which is more responsible, more independent, and therefore capable of greater interdependence. It is a challenge within our lives insofar as it is a call to presence, to the multiple dimensions of that presence which helps us to break out of our usual patterns of seeing and acting, and that leads us to experience the whole and its parts in a new way.

By outlining these priorities, we are merely extending some of the lines of force that already appeared in the description of the external tensions that Palestinian Christians are experiencing. In order to understand those external tensions, we outlined several internal tensions that must be grasped if one is to speak accurately about Palestinian Christians in the concrete situation where they live. But we would want to end this essay with the affirmation that this body of tensions can also come to rest; in the course of its struggle, it can reach a stage where it can get a new grip.

We hope that this essay could be considered such a contribution to the perception of the present stage of struggle. For like Jacob and the angel, we are all wrestling toward the blessing, hidden in the recognition of our names. But there are new names, new recognitions, that still have to be won from forces with which we struggle in the night. By articulating the tensions that comprise the crisis of Palestinian Christians, we hope to contribute to their transformation, if only by helping others to better understand the depth, complexity, and urgency of that crisis. But some readers may realize to what extent some of the more critical tensions have planetary ramifications, and extend not only into the heart of darkness, but also into the purposes of the one who separated light from darkness by his word.

Epilogue

Yehezkel Landau

HEBRON AND JERUSALEM:
CENTERS OF INCLUSIVE HOLINESS

The explosive mix of religion and nationalism fills the evening news broadcasts from the Middle East. We watch the stories and images, and we cringe. Some of us weep. In the land we call holy, everything we hold sacred is being debased by the political misuse of our different religious traditions. When God's name is invoked to justify evil, such desecration must be protested vigorously.

But prophetic outcries are not enough. A counter-vision, an alternative approach to holiness and its impact on our lives, is required to combat the political pollution of Judaism, Islam, or Christianity.

The most agonizing headlines usually come from either Hebron or Jerusalem. The violent confrontations around the shrine of Makhpelah and the temple mount pit Jewish and Muslim believers against one another at places venerated by both traditions. Many Christians who take note of these tragic events may shrug them off as just another example of tribal warfare. But those Christians who take the Bible seriously are apt to view the Israeli-Palestinian conflict through a religious lens. Too often that lens is colored by some theological bias: either a pro-Israel/anti-Islam dualism with apocalyptic overtones, or, conversely, a pro-Palestinian/anti-Zionist stance favoring the weaker, more oppressed side against its alleged oppressor.

In this essay I invite the reader to view the ongoing confrontation between Israelis and Palestinians through another lens, the lens of my own Jewish tradition. That tradition, like any other, has its narrow, even

159

intolerant, aspects. Yet, in addressing the symbolic significance of the two holy cities, Hebron and Jerusalem, Jewish sources offer a lens with a "wide-angle" focus, stretching the tradition beyond its own limitations. The understanding of holiness that emerges may also be a healing anti- dote to the spiritual poison that infects many hearts and minds, even in places far from the Middle East.

The choice of Jerusalem needs little explanation. As *the* city holy to Jews, Christians, and Muslims (albeit for different reasons), it is the sym- bolic heart of "the holy land." But many people, especially Christians, would find Hebron an odd choice as a holy centerpoint. Bethlehem and Nazareth, tied as they are to the life of Jesus, are apt to be higher on the Christian roster of holy places. Partly for this reason, it is worthwhile to focus first on Hebron, and then on Jerusalem.

HEBRON AND MAKHPELAH

As the burial place of Abraham, Sarah, and the other patriarchs and matriarchs (except Rachel, whose grave lies just outside Bethlehem fur- ther north), Hebron symbolizes our common biblical origins. All three monotheistic traditions view Abraham, in particular, as a spiritual fore- father. Indeed, the Hebrew Bible sees Abraham's legacy in universalist terms. God promises him, at the outset of his mission, that "through you all the families of the earth shall be blessed" (Gen 12:3). And when God changes his Hebrew name from *Avram* to *Avraham,* the new name is associated with his destiny as "a father of many nations" (Gen 17:5). The way Abraham relates to God and to other people, and the way he views the land which God has promised to his descendants, have pertinent les- sons for our own time, as we struggle with similar challenges.

Abraham's permanent connection with Hebron comes when Sarah dies. Until then he did not own any property in the land where he and his family had been living for many years. In his dealings with his Hittite neighbors, from whom he wishes to acquire a burial plot for Sarah, he presents himself with utmost humility: "I am a stranger and sojourner together with you" (Gen 23:3).[1] He offers to pay for the property he wants, and negotiates with Ephron over the price in an exchange that reflects the style of bargaining prevalent in the Middle East. Finally he buys the cave of Makhpelah and the area around it for a very high price.

Abraham has already been promised five times by God that his de- scendants would inherit the whole land of Canaan.[2] Had he understood those divine assurances as granting him special rights or privileges in his new homeland, he could have told the Hittites of this special "dispensation" and demanded what was due him. But the patriarch never imposes his "theology" on others in order to gain something, even a plot of land he urgently needs. He knows that covenantal closeness to God does not confer political privilege in human affairs. Just as he demonstrated good will and generosity with his nephew Lot, offering the choicest grazing land when their shepherds were quarreling (Gen 13:7–12), so Abraham treats the Hittites with fraternal respect. He prefers a mutually acceptable agreement over coercive assertion of his own rights.

Abraham's peaceful and generous behavior did not stem from any pacifist orientation. He had, after all, fought to rescue Lot from his kidnapers (Gen 14:12ff). The patriarch simply believed that the way of God, aspiring to justice and righteousness (Gen 18:19), demands respect for the rights of others and a commitment to peacemaking.

Since the Makhpelah cave was Abraham's first real estate acquisition in the land, and he was willing to pay such a high price for it, we are left wondering why he preferred this site over other options. Was it just conveniently close by, or did it possess some special quality known to Abraham? The biblical text does not answer this question. We have to look elsewhere for an explanation, and we find it in the *Zohar* (I, 127ff), the mystical commentary on the five books of Moses. There we learn how Abraham encountered the cave when he ran to catch the calf to feed the three distinguished visitors to his tent (Gen 18:7). According to the story, the calf entered the cave, and Abraham followed it. Smelling the fragrance of paradise, he saw a brilliant light and recognized the ethereal forms of Adam and Eve. At once Abraham realized that this was the burial place of the first human couple, and so it radiated a holiness that transcends all the human distinctions that create division and hostility.

When he discovered the cave's true significance, Abraham understood that this place would best symbolize his own mission and his legacy to future generations. As Rabbi Elie Munk has written:

> . . . every nation has its pantheon, which usually contains the remains of its national heroes and represents a high point of patriotic sentiment. But Abraham, in contrast, wanted to make the Jewish pantheon a symbol of the spirit of universalism. For him, Judaism was the realization of the mission of Adam, of man *par excellence*. . . . This universal character was of the utmost importance for the patriarch. Abraham considered himself the successor and repository of Adam's mission, and he did not hesitate to pay any price . . . in order to assure himself of ownership of the cave wherein the first couple lay buried.[3]

The universal, all-inclusive holiness symbolized by the cave of Makhpelah is reinforced by its very name. "Makhpelah" in Hebrew means "multiplicity." In choosing and acquiring that site, Abraham was affirming a multiple, or pluralistic, understanding of holiness that did not conflict with the monotheism that had been revealed to him. The universal blessing still leaves room for particularities: "Through you all the families of the earth shall be blessed."

To accentuate the inclusive nature of the Makhpelah site, and of Abraham's legacy, the biblical story tells of Ishmael's return from the desert when the patriarch dies. Together with Isaac, Ishmael buries their common father in the holy cave (Gen 25:9). No specific act of reconciliation between the two half-brothers is recounted, unlike the emotional reunion between Jacob and Esau later; yet the fact that Ishmael is not cast away for good has historical significance extending throughout the centuries, until today.

In Jewish tradition, Ishmael is viewed as the progenitor of the Arab peoples. The twelve princes destined to arise from his descendants (Gen 17:20) are a parallel to the twelve tribes of Israel. The children of Ishmael and the children of Israel, like Abraham's two sons, grew apart while retaining their deep identification with their patriarchal ancestor. The "Israelites" of today are the Jews, while the vast majority of the Ishmaelite Arabs are now Muslims. (This statement in no way denigrates the importance of non-Muslim Arab believers, including Arab Christians.) The Jewish and Islamic traditions have so much in common, and the Hebrew and Arabic languages are so similar, that it is natural to ask why Jews and Muslims in Hebron today cannot recognize their commonalities, instead of competing for the Abrahamic blessing at the very spot where the patriarch lies buried.

The name "Hebron," or *Hevron* in Hebrew, derives from the same linguistic root as *haver,* or "friend." The Arabic name for the city, *Al-Khalil,* also means "the friend," referring to Abraham, the beloved friend of God. Whether we call him *Avraham Avinu* or *Abbuna Ibrahim,* he *is* our common father. But so long as our faith traditions are exploited by militant nationalists, Abraham's memory, and everything he taught, will be defiled. And friendly, fraternal relations between Jews and Arabs will remain an elusive dream, in Hebron and everywhere else.

Both peoples will have to make sacrifices if the blessing is to be shared and a genuine peace achieved. The Muslim Palestinians in Al-Khalil will have to accept a Jewish community in their midst, as was always the case until the horrible massacre of 1929. From 1948 until 1967, when Jordan occupied the West Bank, Jews could not even visit Hebron. The Jewish return to the city came with the Israeli military victory in June of 1967. Unfortunately, most of the Jews who have taken up residence in Hebron since then have not come in the humble, gracious manner that Abraham demonstrated. Instead, they have exacerbated a situation made already tense and hostile by the harsh realities of military occupation.

To move from hostile confrontation to truly friendly and mutually beneficial relations, Israeli Jews will have to make a painful sacrifice of their own. As part of a peace agreement that ensures Israel's security, they will have to relinquish control over Hebron and the rest of the West Bank so that the Palestinian majority there can enjoy freedom and self-determination under their own government. For any religious Jew, this is a sacrifice tantamount to amputating a part of our collective Jewish body. A symbolic Israeli presence might remain, perhaps through a consulate or diplomatic mission located within the civilian Jewish quarter of the city. But the Israeli army will have to withdraw, and the Palestinian government which eventually rules there will have to undertake to protect the Jewish minority and service its needs. Under such an arrangement, the prayers of both communities within the common Makhpelah shrine may become sincere affirmations of justice and righteousness and, in that way, truly hallow Abraham's memory.

JERUSALEM: HEALING THE HEART

If relinquishing control over Hebron is like an amputation for most Israeli Jews, then any thought of negotiating over the status of Jerusalem is like contemplating open-heart surgery. In either case, the operation would be willingly undergone only if the medical diagnosis leaves no alternative. Jerusalem is, indeed, the heart of "the holy land" for Jews, Christians, and Muslims. It beats to the rhythm of ancient traditions and gives vitality to eternal hopes.

Any objective examination of the social reality in Jerusalem today would detect signs of serious coronary disease. If we were to imagine the four quarters of the Old City as the four chambers of a heart, we would have to acknowledge that the flow of people and cultural life from one section to another is chronically blocked. The barriers of ignorance, fear, suspicion, and hatred severely hamper the organic functioning of the holy city.

As in the case of Hebron, Jewish tradition offers insights that could alleviate—perhaps even cure—the ailments that afflict Jerusalem. And

Jerusalem, like Hebron, is in many ways a microcosm of the entire Israeli-Palestinian dilemma. We must be very careful, however, in proposing political remedies for Jerusalem. Bodies can survive amputations, but not a mistake during open-heart surgery. Some have likened Israel and Palestine to two Siamese twins joined together; if so, then the fact that they share a common heart makes their separation especially problematic and delicate. Whatever political surgery results from a negotiated peace, it must allow for Jerusalem to remain a single, undivided heart nourishing the bodies of both peoples.

No clear precedent for such a sharing of Jerusalem exists in Jewish sources or Jewish history. But the Torah does include teachings about the holy city that emphasize its inclusive and reconciling dimension. The messianic visions in Isaiah 2, Micah 4, and Zechariah 8 are well-known passages describing a time of universal peace. Jerusalem, sometimes called Zion, is also the subject of many familiar psalms. Psalm 122 is one of them:

I was glad when they said to me,
Let us go into the house of the Lord;
when our feet stood within thy gates, O Jerusalem!
Jerusalem, built as a city
whose parts are linked together;
there the tribes used to go up,
the tribes of the Lord,
an appointed practice for Israel,
to give thanks to the name of the Lord.
For there are set thrones of judgment,
the thrones of the house of David.
Pray for the peace of Jerusalem:
they who love you shall prosper,
peace be within your sanctuary,
and prosperity within your palaces.
For the sake of my brothers and friends,
I will say,
Peace be within you;
for the sake of the house of the Lord our God,
I will seek your good.

The psalm refers to the union of the different Israelite tribes brought about by this capital city from the time of King David. The two spheres of Jewish national life, the political and the spiritual, are also alluded to: the "thrones of judgment," "the house of David," and "your palaces" all refer to the kingship, the temporal authority, while "your sanctuary" and "the house of the Lord our God" refer to the holy temple and the role of the priests. It is Jerusalem's function, part of its essential character, to integrate these two spheres.

Neither Jewish tradition nor Islam can conceive of a "secular" society divorcing religion from politics; such a social order would be like a physical body without a soul. Christianity's tendency to separate the spiritual from the temporal realm has led to a focus on a "celestial Jerusalem" existing in another dimension—or, metaphorically, in the human heart—with no necessary connection to the earthly city called Jerusalem. (Paradoxically, that earthly city continues to attract Christian pilgrims from all over the world.) For the Hebrew prophets, Jerusalem was both a reality and a symbol. The actual, terrestrial Jerusalem is the place which Isaiah prophesied would become a unifying spiritual center, with "a house of prayer for all peoples" established there (Is 56:7).

Since the destruction of the second temple, Jewish prayer and pilgrimage have been directed toward Jerusalem. The capital of the reestablished Jewish state could not be any other city but Jerusalem. The challenge now for Jews is whether we can accept Jerusalem serving as the spiritual and political center for another people, the Palestinian people.

The Arabic name for the city, *Al-Quds,* "the Holy," reflects Islam's view of Jerusalem as the third holiest site, after Mecca and Medina. Since classical Islam, like Judaism, views religion and politics as inseparable spheres of life, it is unreasonable to expect the Palestinians (ninety-five percent of whom are Muslims) to accept another city as their national capital. The question for the Palestinians is whether they, in turn, can accept a sovereign Jewish state with Jerusalem as *its* capital. Many Muslims, as well as some Christians, have not yet integrated that reality within the framework of their faith or historical understanding.

The common challenge to all three faiths is to broaden their understanding of monotheism to allow for plurality and diversity within the plan of the one God: the idea, again, of Makhpelah, multiplicity within a unifying whole. Abraham, our common forefather, grasped this simple yet profound truth. In his own lifetime there was already a monotheistic presence in Jerusalem, under the leadership of Melchizedek (Gen 14:18–20). Abraham receives a blessing from Melchizedek, who was ruler and high priest of the city when it was still called *Shalem.* Melchizedek's dual role of priest-king indicates that the integration of spiritual and political authority was part of Jerusalem's character even before the patriarchal period. Abraham's acceptance of Melchizedek's blessing affirms his understanding that worship of the one supreme God can take different forms, something we have yet to appreciate many centuries later.

A famous rabbinic midrash (*Genesis Rabbah* 56.10) bases itself on the Abraham-Melchizedek encounter, as well as on the *akedah* drama in Genesis 22, to trace the origin of the name *Yerushalayim,* Hebrew for "Jerusalem." After Abraham sacrifices the ram as a substitute for the spared Isaac, he gives the place (Mount Moriah, the future site of the holy temple) his own name: *Adonai yireh.* The biblical text itself explains this name as "the Lord, or the Eternal, will appear" on that mountain (Gen 22:14). The midrash has God combining the two words associated with Abraham and Melchizedek, *yireh* and *Shalem,* to make *Yeru-Shalem.* This new, inclusive name represents a combination of two distinct monotheistic realities in the persons of Abraham and Melchizedek, a valuable insight for the situation we face today. For in this midrashic parable lies an understanding of holiness, from God's perspective, that allows pluralism to exist and flourish on a common monotheistic foundation. The addition of the second letter *yod* to make the plural ending, *Yerushala-yim,* suggests a multiplicity, like *Makhpelah,* that joins together discrete elements within a transcendent sanctity.

Another play on the name Jerusalem/*Yerushalayim* is *Ir Shalom,* the "City of Peace." *Shalem* means "whole," and the essence of true peace, *shalom,* is the reconciliation of diverse, even opposing, elements within a harmonious whole. So it is with each of us, as conflicted personalities yearning for inner peace; and so it is with any society, fractured by competing groups and interests. The idea of a healing, reconciling wholeness appears in the rules for constructing the altar within the holy temple. Built on the same spot where Abraham bound Isaac and, instead, sacrificed the ram, the altar atoned for human sins, including the sin of violence. Even when violence may be a lesser evil, as in repelling aggression, it is still a sin to be atoned for. For this reason, the altar had to be made from whole, uncut stones (*avanim shlemot*). No metal instrument that might, under other circumstances, serve as a weapon was permitted to touch them.

The builder of the first temple, Solomon, had a Hebrew name, *Shlomo,* that derives from the same root denoting wholeness and peace. He was given the task of constructing the holy temple after his father, King David, was denied this privilege by God. The reason for this prohibition was that David was "a man of wars and had shed blood" (1 Chr 28:3). He had fought wars that he had to fight; yet this violent past made him unsuitable to be the builder of the Lord's house. And the threshing floor of

Aravna the Jebusite, on which the holy of holies would rest, was purchased by David, not conquered (2 Sam 24:21ff)—a non-violent parallel to Abraham's purchase of the cave of Makhpelah.

If such a great figure as David was disqualified from fulfilling one of his dearest longings because he had engaged in violence, how perverse are the apocalyptic fantasies, shared by some Jews and some Christians, that anticipate the violent removal of the Muslim shrines from the temple mount (in Arabic, *Al-Haram es-Sharif*) and the erection of a third temple in their place. Such dangerous notions demonstrate how our spirituality can be warped by an *ex*clusive, rather than an *in*clusive, sense of what holiness means.

Another inclusive vision of Jerusalem's sanctity is presented in Psalm 87:

> His foundation is in the holy mountains.
> The Lord loves the gates of Zion
> more than all the dwellings of Jacob.
> Glorious things are spoken of you, O city of God. *Selah*
> I will make mention of Rahab and Babylon
> to those who know me;
> behold Philistia, and Tyre, with Ethiopia, saying,
> This man was born there.
> But of Zion it shall be said,
> This and that man were born in her,
> and the highest himself shall establish her.
> The Lord shall record,
> when he registers the peoples,
> that this man was born there. *Selah*
> And singers and dancers alike shall say,
> All my springs are in you.

Here the imagery is feminine: Zion as the holy mother city, with an infinitely expansive maternity roster. Other cities and countries are identified with specific group identities, but Jerusalem is all-inclusive. All believers are born in her: so God himself shall record. The complementary masculine and feminine language corresponds to the Jewish mystical understanding of the transcendent Father God and the feminine *shekhinah* presence indwelling on earth and "at home" in Jerusalem. If Abraham is our common forefather, then Jerusalem is our common mother, home to the *shekhinah,* which has the capacity to bless and nourish an infinite number of God's children from her sacred, ever-flowing fountains.

This is a lovely poetic image. But how can we experience such an inclusive sense of the divine presence embracing and blessing us all? Jerusalem today seems so far from that reality, with her inhabitants caught in the grip of terrible fear. The political pollution is so great that the sublime poetry of Psalm 87 either rings hollow or becomes contaminated by partisan associations. Palestinian Christians, for example, cannot recite this psalm without choking on the word "Zion," which they identify with Zionism and the modern state of Israel, their enemy. Israeli Jews, for their part, may read some of the psalms in a triumphalistic spirit, inflating their pride at the expense of others. These reflex orientations, conditioned by years of conflict, are symptomatic of the spiritual disease afflicting Jerusalem today. Clearly a fair political settlement is necessary for the healing of souls, no less than bodies.

PLURALISTIC GEOGRAPHY: ARMENIANS, JEWS, PALESTINIANS

If we return to the metaphor of Jerusalem as the heart, the diseased but nonetheless holy heart, a healing path to justice and peace may lead through the pluralistic geography of her four quarters.

The ecumenical "Christian Quarter" resonates with the diversity of Christian life in Jerusalem over the centuries. I will leave it to Christians to decide whether this diversity is a positive sign of "multiplicity" within the Christian family, or whether the separate chapels within the Church of the Holy Sepulchre signify a lamentable fragmentation among the different Christian communities.

One Christian community has a separate quarter unto itself: the Armenians. They were the first people to adopt Christianity en masse as their national faith, in the year 301. The Armenians are a deeply devout people, and their small Jerusalem community (numbering some fifteen hundred people) is centered around the ornate Cathedral of Saint James. When one considers the distinctness of Armenian Christians, the unique features of their history and faith, and then juxtaposes them to the Israeli Jews and the Palestinian Muslims in adjacent quarters, a remarkable pattern reveals itself.

These three peoples, the Armenians, the Jews, and the Palestinians, are rooted in the holy land for centuries with their respective identities and traditions. One common aspect of their religious heritages is a three-fold loyalty: to a people, to a faith tradition, and to a particular land. Perhaps because of this shared basis for self-identification, the three peoples have undergone similar experiences, particularly in this twentieth century.

On the level of the physical body, all three communities have endured traumatic massacres: first the Armenian genocide before and during World War I; then we Jews passed through the valley of death during World War II; and since then the Palestinians have suffered massacres at the hands of virtually every other Middle Eastern people they have encountered. The Palestinian experience cannot be objectively compared with the genocide of the Jews or of the Armenians; yet a *subjective* sense of being survivor peoples, mourning their martyrs and affirming their communal dignity, does characterize all three communities.

The three peoples share yet another common denominator: all have suffered, in this century, exile from their respective homelands. This is more an assault to the spirit than to the physical body. We Jews, of course, know what it means to be refugees, "strangers in strange lands," for more than twenty centuries. Now if, in this twentieth century, we have been blessed to return to Jerusalem as a free people, and we rejoice over that homecoming, while the Armenian and Palestinian communities are suffering the pain of their own diasporas, there must be some lesson in this fateful intermingling of joy and sorrow.

One image that conveys the shared experience is of three traumatized individuals walking through darkness while holding candles, lit by their ancestors, to illuminate their way. Each of the three wanderers longs for his lost homeland. Each of them fears that, out of the darkness, some enemy will attack him, making him a victim once again. None of the three is able to trust others who might help him overcome the trauma and the dread. Then, suddenly, the three of them converge, and their candles illumine each other's faces. Each experiences the shock of mutual recognition. And in the human faces is a reflection of something mysteriously divine, so that each can echo the wondrous exclamation of the wounded Jacob, renamed Israel: ". . . for I have truly seen your face as though seeing the face of God" (Gen 33:10).

An awareness of the divine aspect of each other's identity would help us overcome our conditioned fears, loyalties, and hatreds. The pluralistic sacred geography that includes Armenian Christians, Israeli Jews, and Palestinian Muslims and Christians may hold a key to one of humanity's most pressing challenges: how to simultaneously honor particularities *and* commonalities in human relations. Abraham's words to the Hittites have a broader meaning: we are all "strangers and sojourners" on this earth, sharing it for a time with other children of God. Elsewhere in the Torah, the implications of this fundamental truth are made clear. Moses teaches, in connection with the sabbatical year, that "the land shall not be sold forever; for the land is mine (says the Lord, and) you are strangers and sojourners with me" (Lev 25:23). In other words, we belong to the land through the grace of God; the land does not belong to us. And King David, in his farewell blessing to the people before passing the kingship over to Solomon, humbly acknowledges our human frailty and mortality: "For we are all strangers before you, and sojourners, as were all our forefathers; our days on earth are as a shadow, and there is no abiding" (1 Chr 29:15).

Out of such humility and praise may come the fraternal consciousness that can make Hebron/Al-Khalil and Jerusalem/Al-Quds the centers of reconciliation they are meant to be. The underlying, liberating truth is that the one creator has made us all in the divine image, every human being infinitely precious and beloved. Here on earth, our common father Abraham and our mother city Jerusalem make all of us sisters and brothers in the family of believers. If we could recognize one another in that spirit, we could truly work together to sanctify God's holy land and share the divine blessing of *shalom.*

NOTES

1. The great medieval commentator Rashi has two interpretations of this verse. The evident meaning (*pshat* in Hebrew) is: "I am a stranger having come from another land, but I have settled among you." A midrashic explanation which he brings is: "If you agree to sell me the land, then I will regard myself as a stranger and will pay for it; but if not, then I shall claim it as a settler and will take it as my legal right, because the Holy One, Blessed be He, has said to me (Gen 12:7), 'Unto your seed will I give this land.' " This midrashic interpretation does not seem to square with Abraham's conduct, here and elsewhere; and, as we shall see at the end of this essay, two other biblical verses using the combined form of "stranger and settler/sojourner" (*ger vetoshav*) offer humility, not claims to privilege or superiority, as the intended ideal.

2. Cf. Gen 12:7; 13:15; 15:7; 15:18; 17:8.

3. Elie Munk, *The Call of the Torah* (Jerusalem and New York: Feldheim, 1980), Vol. I, pp. 492–93.

Notes on the Contributors

His Grace Archbishop SHAHÉ AJAMIAN is a member of the Supreme Synod of the Armenian Church. He also is a member of the Central Committee of the World Council of Churches. His Grace was at one time dean of the Armenian Patriarchate's Theological Seminary and has taught philosophy and Armenian church history.

PETER DU BRUL, S.J. teaches religion at Bethlehem University, the Latin Patriarchate Seminary in Beit Jalla, and the international program in biblical formation of the Sisters of Sion, Jerusalem.

DAVID BURRELL, C.S.C. is professor of philosophy and theology at the University of Notre Dame. After serving as rector of the Ecumenical Institute for Theological Research (Tantur) in Jerusalem, he has taken up a comparative study of Jewish, Christian, and Islamic philosophical theology: *Knowing the Unknowable God. Avicenna, Maimonides, and Aquinas.* He is also the author of *Aquinas: God and Action, Exercises in Religious Understanding,* numerous articles and, most recently, a translation of Al-Ghazālī's treatise on the ninety-nine names of God.

MARCEL DUBOIS, O.P. has lived in Israel for over twenty-five years and became an Israeli citizen in 1974. He taught philosophy at the Hebrew University serving as department head from 1980–1985 and has for many years advised the Vatican on Catholic-Jewish relations. He is active in the Ecumenical Theological Research Fraternity in Israel, editing its journal *Immanuel.*

171

YEHEZKEL LANDAU is executive director of "Oz veShalom-Netivot Shalom," the religious peace movement in Israel. He teaches Judaism and interfaith relations at the Tantur Ecumenical Institute, at St. George's Anglican College, and the program in biblical formation of the Sisters of Sion in Jerusalem. A graduate of Harvard Divinity School (M.T.S.), he received that school's Distinguished Alumnus Award in 1990. Among his published articles are "Blessing Both Jew and Palestinian: A Religious Zionist Perspective" (*The Christian Century*); "Martyrdom in Paul's Religious Ethics: An Exegetical Commentary on Romans 5:7" (*Immanuel*); and "Shuttling Between Heaven and Earth: Rabbi Adin Steinsaltz" (*Ariel* magazine).

ANDRÉ NEHER (1914–1988) was director of the department of Jewish studies at Strasbourg University. He also served as vice president of L'Amitié Judéo-Chrétienne and president of the French section of the World Jewish Congress before moving to Jerusalem. One of the leading Jewish thinkers of this century, he published many books, among them *Moses and the Vocation of the Jews, The Prophetic Existence, Biblical History of the People of Israel,* and *The Exile of the Word.*

PINCHAS HACOHEN PELI (d. 1989) was professor of Jewish thought and literature at the Ben-Gurion University of the Negev at the time of his death. His books include *Abraham Joshua Heschel: An Intellectual Biography, On Repentance: The Thought and Oral Discourses of Rabbi Joseph B. Soloveitchick* (Paulist Press) and *Torah Today.*

SIMON SCHOON is chairman of the Dutch Council of Christians and Jews, and was for ten years responsible for Christian-Jewish relations in the Dutch Reformed Church. He served for six and a half years as pastor of the Nes Ammim ecumenical Christian community in western Galilee.

Index of Authors and Subjects

Clemens Thoma and Michael Wyschogrod, editors, *Parable and Story in Judaism and Christianity* (A Stimulus Book, 1989).

Eugene J. Fisher and Leon Klenicki, editors, *In Our Time: The Flowering of Jewish–Catholic Dialogue* (A Stimulus Book, 1990).

Leon Klenicki, editor, *Toward a Theological Encounter* (A Stimulus Book, 1991).

John Rousmaniere, *A Bridge to Dialogue: The Story of Jewish-Christian Relations* (A Stimulus Book, 1991).

STIMULUS BOOKS are developed by Stimulus Foundation, a not-for-profit organization, and are published by Paulist Press. The Foundation wishes to further the publication of scholarly books on Jewish and Christian topics that are of importance to Judaism and Christianity.

Stimulus Foundation was established by an erstwhile refugee from Nazi Germany who intends to contribute with these publications to the improvement of communication between Jews and Christians.

Books for publication in this Series will be selected by a committee of the Foundation, and offers of manuscripts and works in progress should be addressed to:

Stimulus Foundation
785 West End Ave.
New York, N.Y. 10025